CHRISTMAS IN CANADA

CHRISTMAS IN CANADA

Christmas Around the World
From World Book

World Book, Inc.
a Scott Fetzer company

CHICAGO   LONDON   SYDNEY   TORONTO

STAFF

Publisher Emeritus
William H. Nault

President
Daniel C. Wasp

EDITORIAL

Managing Editor
Maureen Mostyn Liebenson

Associate Editor
Karen Zack Ingebretsen

Permissions Editor
Janet T. Peterson

Director of Research
Mary Norton

Researchers
Susan Clendenin
Lynn Durbin

ART

Executive Director
Roberta Dimmer

Art Director
Wilma Stevens

Senior Designers
Lisa Buckley
Deirdre Wroblewski

Cover Designer
Brenda Tropinski

Senior Photographs Editor
Sandra Dyrlund

PRODUCT PRODUCTION

Vice President, Production and Technology
Daniel N. Bach

Director of Manufacturing/Pre-press
Sandra Van den Broucke

Manufacturing Manager
Barbara Podczerwinski

Production Manager
Randi Park

Proofreaders
Anne Dillon
Daniel J. Marotta

DIRECT MARKETING

Marketing Manager
John Deneen

Product Development Director
Paul Kobasa

World Book, Inc.
525 W. Monroe
Chicago, IL 60661

ISBN: 0-7166-0894-4
LC: 94-60826

Printed in the United States of America
1 2 3 4 5 6 7 8 9 10 99 98 97 96 95 94

World Book wishes to thank the following individuals for their contributions to *Christmas in Canada:* Dorothy Duncan, Anna Eliuk, Sarah Figlio, Ellen Hughes, Olive Koyama, and Heather Mills.

Contents

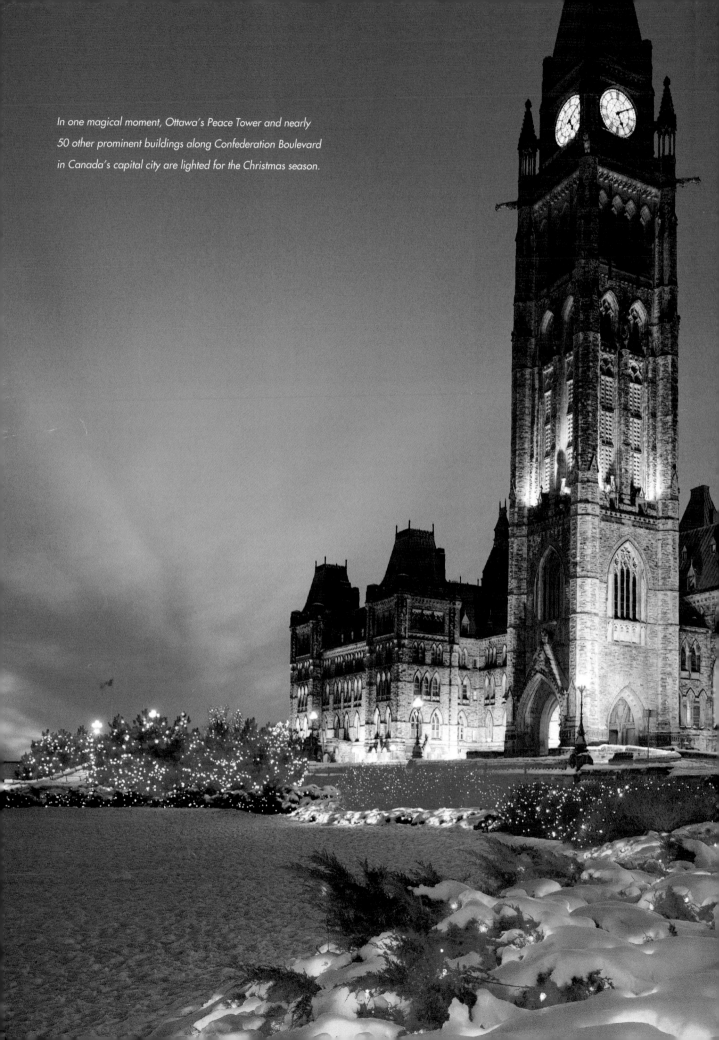

In one magical moment, Ottawa's Peace Tower and nearly 50 other prominent buildings along Confederation Boulevard in Canada's capital city are lighted for the Christmas season.

BIG CITIES AND SMALL TOWNS CELEBRATE THE SEASON

Canada is the country where Christmas came to stay. Beginning more than 400 years ago, age-old Christmas traditions from countries around the world have made their way to Canada along with great numbers of immigrant families. And here those cherished customs have prospered—and have been adopted by others.

The people of Canada are proud of the spirit of good will and understanding that brings their citizens from such different cultural backgrounds as French, English, German, Ukrainian, and First Nations together as one people—Canadians. And there is no better time to display both the diversity and the unity of these peoples than during the Christmas season.

In this Christmas-card wonderland of a country with its snowy woods, frozen ponds, and northern lights, people from various cultures have discovered a place where differences are celebrated and Christmas traditions abound.

CHRISTMAS LIGHTS ACROSS CANADA

Each year since 1986, on the first Thursday in December, thousands of Christmas lights that adorn government buildings across Canada are illuminated at one moment. This dazzling display symbolically unites Canadians nationwide in a glorious celebration of Christmas.

At the national Christmas Lights Across Canada lighting ceremony in Ottawa on that night, the governor general of Canada flips a switch at exactly 6:55 p.m., sending a glow into the cold winter night from more than 150,000 lights. The brilliant tiny bulbs together illuminate the Parliament Buildings and nearly 50 other important national institutions along Confederation Boulevard, Canada's ceremonial route. The lights will remain aglow each night throughout the Christmas season.

At the moment the switch is flipped in Ottawa, a government leader in each provincial or territorial capital across Canada also switches on Christmas lights, bringing all the individual celebrations together. In the nation's capital, video messages from provincial and territorial leaders add Christmas greetings from each part of the country to the national ceremony.

Across this vast country, provincial and territorial lighting ceremonies proudly reflect the distinctive character of their regions as they join with others to light Canada in festive celebration of the season.

In Charlottetown, capital of the tiny Maritime province of Prince Edward Island, city residents enjoy a Christmas Lights Across Canada ceremony rich in history and tradition. In the center of town, colorful lights shine out on that special December night before historic Province House, considered the birthplace of Canada. It was at the confederation meeting at Province House in 1864 that Canada became a country. Charlottetown's own town crier is on hand to announce the arriving premier, lieutenant governor, and other dignitaries, and many community members turn out in Victorian garb for the occasion. There is a choir performance and community caroling session, plus hot cider and shortbread or fruitcake for the holiday crowd. Just before the lights at Province House are switched on, every person in attendance receives a candle to hold high. In the capital, with a population of only 20,000,

At Christmas Lights Across Canada ceremonies everywhere, Canadians help light the night. Here, a boys' choir in Halifax raises candles and voices in celebration.

approximately 500 people turn out each December to represent Prince Edward Island in the ceremony uniting Canadians everywhere at Christmastime.

In the east coast capital of Fredericton, New Brunswick, the premier hosts an annual tree-lighting ceremony at the grand old Legislative Assembly building, seat of the provincial government. As he flips a switch, all of downtown Fredericton is lighted for the holidays. To the delight of Fredericton's children, Santa is on hand this night to distribute "barley toys" and "chicken bones," traditional Maritime

Christmas candies, to the gathered crowd.

A second tree-lighting ceremony is held this night in front of Fredericton's historic City Hall, where a colorfully adorned balsam fir, New Brunswick's official tree, shines brilliantly when Fredericton's mayor officiates. Residents who brave the cold to share in Fredericton's celebration enjoy hot apple cider and a second visit from Santa, bringing candy canes this time, as they warm the night with Christmas carols.

Far across Canada in the great plains capital of Regina, Saskatchewan, the Christmas

In joining the national Christmas lights celebration, each province or territory reveals its own special charm. The elegant Legislative Assembly Building in Fredericton provides a historical setting for New Brunswick's provincial ceremony.

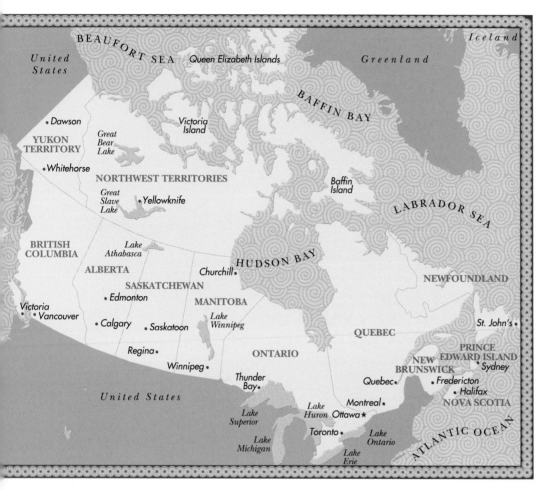

candy canes are served, and the crowd is welcomed inside to tour the decorated Legislative Building and witness a live Nativity pageant.

In the country's far, frigid northwest, where Christmastime temperatures are typically –20 to –50 °F (–29 to –46 °C), the small gathering of residents in the Yukon capital of Whitehorse are welcomed inside to share in the territory's intimate Christmas Lights Across Canada ceremony at the Yukon Government Administration Building. Here, to connect with the rest of Canada, the lighting ceremony is held in the late afternoon. While one large tree glows in colored lights outside the building, five more trees inside are lighted all at once to fill the building with Christmas cheer. The focus is on children in this close-knit Yukon community's ceremony. Children's choirs or bands perform for the event, and each child receives a traditional treat bag filled with candies, cookies, and fruit. The joy of celebration continues in the days approaching Christmas, as the lighting ceremony opens a season of daily Christmas shows, and townspeople are welcomed to stop by

From St. John's, Newfoundland, to Vancouver, British Columbia, from Whitehorse in the Yukon Territory to Ottawa, Ontario, Christmas Lights Across Canada unites Canadians in small towns and big cities in a dazzling celebration of the season.

Lights Across Canada ceremony links the city's thousands of Regina Sparkles lights to the united Canadian celebration. Begun several years ago as a Christmas lights contest, Regina Sparkles has grown to an all-city celebration as lighting displays shine out from homes and businesses on every street. As they stand before the Saskatchewan Legislative Building on that dark December night to join their bright lights to the countrywide celebration, Regina residents sing carols, hold candles and light sticks in the air, and shout out "Merry Christmas, Canada!" The traditional hot cider and the administration building to see a variety of local performers.

For all their regional and cultural differences, there is a powerful national pride uniting Canadians, especially at Christmas. At every provincial or territorial Christmas Lights Across Canada gathering, the thousands of Canadians who brave the cold to witness these ceremonies are given candles so that they can add their own light to the glow of a united Canadian Christmas.

CHURCH SERVICES ACROSS CANADA

A deeply religious country with strong Anglican and Catholic traditions, Canada is aglow on Christmas Eve with the celebration of Christ's birth. Many world-famous Canadian churches offer special Christmas services.

St. Michael's Cathedral in Toronto features one of the few remaining boys' choirs. The choir's remarkable singing is the highlight at a special midnight Mass on Christmas Eve.

The Church of the Transfiguration, outside Toronto in suburban Markham, is open to the public only on special occasions; naturally, Christmas is one of them. On this holy day, the church draws thousands to its Christmas service. Built just a few years ago, this very large, onion-domed church has bells only slightly smaller than those of Notre Dame Cathedral in France and was consecrated by the Pope at its first Mass.

Overlooking the sparkling lights of Montreal, St. Joseph's Oratory features a collection of Nativity scenes from around the world. The Christmas Eve service at this beautiful shrine is a much-loved tradition for thousands in Montreal.

Montreal's other world-famous church, Notre-Dame Basilica, boasts a 5,772-pipe organ and an exquisite, carved-wood sanctuary. The parish celebrates Christmas Eve *messe de minuit* (midnight Mass) with hymns and carols in the clear, pure tones of its children's choir.

Notre-Dame Basilica in Montreal holds a special place in the hearts of city residents. Here, thousands of worshipers come each Christmas Eve to attend the messe de minuit and hear the basilica's children's choir.

THE CANADIAN TREE

One version of Christmas history places the first decorated Canadian tree in the home of a German immigrant family in Sorel, Quebec, in 1781, where it was trimmed with pine cones, feathers, and Indian crafts. Other sources say the first tree was set up in Halifax in 1846 by William Pryor, a local merchant, for his German-born wife, who decorated it with German glass ornaments.

This much is sure: In Canada, trees could be found to inspire any decorator. In the abundant woods of Nova Scotia and other parts of eastern Canada, early settlers discovered a Christmas treasure, the tall, richly colored, sweet-scented balsam fir. While Christmas trees in England were often small and delicate, suited for a tabletop, here was a Canadian tree that would stand tall, lending its stature and scent to the entire room.

In the 1750's, German immigrants settled in the rich woods of Lunenburg County, Nova Sco-

tia. Here, they began to chop balsam firs from the woods around them, using teams of paired oxen to drag out heavy loads of Christmas trees. Today, the distant jingle of ox bells can still be heard in the woods as a remnant core of Lunenburg County families continue to employ oxen and chop trees with an ax, carrying on their family's long-time tradition. Joining them all around are modern foresters with power saws, mechanical loaders and conveyors, and advanced harvesting and replanting techniques, for the Canadian balsam is big business at Christmas.

Nova Scotia, rightly named "The Christmas Tree Province," produces more than 1.5 million trees each year for eastern Canada and the United States. While 90 percent of the market is concentrated in the United States and in Canada's eastern provinces, trees from Nova Scotia are shipped as far as Central America, the Caribbean, and Venezuela.

The second largest supplier

of Christmas trees among the provinces is Quebec, followed by New Brunswick, Ontario, and British Columbia. In all, Canadian tree growers market approximately 6 million Christmas trees every year.

Balsam fir trees are a Canadian specialty, growing in the eastern provinces and in only a few of the most northern U.S. states, which share Canada's frosty fall weather. This is because sweet-scented balsams love the cold. A full 15 nights of hard frost are needed before a balsam will hold its needles after being cut. Harvesting for the offshore market begins each year on November 1, with later dates set for markets nearer to Canada.

Each year, one very special 70-foot (21-meter) tree is selected from the Nova Scotia woods to be presented to the city of Boston, Massachusetts. The reason for the gift dates back to 1917, when a ship carrying a full load of explosives blew up in Halifax Harbour, killing 1,900 people instantly and destroying

much of the city. While help poured in from around the world, it was the tremendous generosity and volunteer assistance of the people of Boston that touched the heart of Halifax. Since 1973, Halifax has shown its gratitude by giving Boston its beautiful central tree each year. Placed in Boston's Prudential Square and decorated with thousands of colorful lights, the giant balsam stands as a symbol of friendship between the cities.

In the late 1800's, early conservationists were alarmed that the tremendous popularity of the Christmas tree might deplete the forests of Nova Scotia.

A popular women's magazine proposed that families display their gifts on a gaily decorated stepladder instead or simply leave them out on the breakfast table. But the editors had underestimated both North America's love for the Christmas tree and the richness of the Canadian woods.

Today, more than 30,000 acres (12,140 hectares) in Nova Scotia alone and a total of approximately 100,000 acres (40,468 hectares) in Canada are committed to Christmas tree production. While the market demand for the deliciously scented balsam fir grows yearly, so do more trees.

The woods of Nova Scotia are so fertile that after hundreds of years of Christmas celebrations, Christmas trees are still being cut from naturally established forests where new trees quickly spring up to replace those cut. In Nova Scotia and in other provinces, well-planned conservation and replanting programs also help keep pace, assuring the continuing beauty of the woods and a bounty of tall, richly green Canadian trees for Christmases to come.

In Canada, settlers found the perfect Christmas tree.

In Canada, winter sports and Christmas are a perfect pair. In Quebec City, children line up for a thrilling toboggan ride at Château Frontenac.

A FRENCH~CANADIAN CHRISTMAS

■

Christmas first came to Canada in the hearts of adventuring Frenchmen. Often traveling alone, French hunters were the first Europeans to trap and trade in the bountiful Canadian woods. French missionaries bravely followed in the hunters' footsteps, bringing the teachings of Christianity—and Christmas—to the native peoples they encountered.

Viking ships are said to have visited the Atlantic coast of Canada nearly 1,000 years ago. In the summer of 1497, John Cabot touched shore at Newfoundland and claimed the territory for England. Soon after Cabot's discovery, European companies began making annual expeditions to the fertile fishing grounds of the Grand Banks off Newfoundland's coast.

Still, it was the French who took the lead in exploring Canada. French explorer Samuel de Champlain established a permanent settlement, founding the city of Quebec in 1608. French trappers and traders were the first to explore Canada's deep woods.

Today, French Canadians—descendants of those early French explorers, trappers, and settlers—comprise 25 percent of Canada's population.

EARLY CHRISTMAS CELEBRATIONS

In years past, the religious celebration of Christmas for French Canadians began at the close of November, on the first Sunday of Advent—and so did the work. Weeks of preparation were needed to ready the array of offerings for the sumptuous Christmas feast, the New Year's Day celebration, and the week of parties and hungry visitors in between.

In this famous lithograph, artist Edmond J. Massicotte depicts early Quebec settlers returning home from the messe de minuit to réveillon, the dinner at the heart of their Christmas celebration.

First came the meats—beef, pork, chicken, wild game, partridges, and turkeys—to be readied for pies, stews, and soups. Then, dozens upon dozens of doughnuts were fried, tossed in sugar, stored in fresh laundered pillowcases, and hung in the meat freezer. And there they would hang until a long-awaited Christmas Eve.

Preparing the food for Christmas was more fun than work. In times past, a taffy pull party, held on November 25 in honor of Saint Catherine, the patron saint of single women, was one of the first delights of the Christmas season. Presented as a working session to prepare candy for Christmas, taffy pulls offered a chance for eligible bachelors and single young women from farms all around the area to get to know each other before the rush of Christmas parties.

After weeks of anticipation and preparation, Christmas arrived for French Canadians with *la messe de minuit*, the midnight Mass on Christmas Eve. Earlier in the evening, young children would hang stockings and climb into bed. The older children and other family members would then decorate the Christmas tree with lights, golden angels, and garlands of silver. They then would place a small Nativity scene or crèche under the tree. In fact, the Nativity scene—a cherished Christmas tradition today throughout North America—was introduced to Canadians by French settlers.

Soon it would be time to venture off to church. When recalling Christmases past, many French Canadians tell of fond memories of being awakened by their parents, bundled into warm clothes, and carried off into the frigid, starry night to the wonders of this Mass. The feeling inspired was powerful.

Gazing at the church's carved wood warmed by candlelight, the dazzling stained-glass windows, and the figures of the life-sized crèche, those attending the service sang beloved carols and listened to the story of the Christ child's birth. Traditionally, there were three Masses on this night: the first and most solemn, Night Mass; the Dawn Mass; and the Day Mass. These church services extended the re-ligious celebration into the light of Christmas Day.

RÉVEILLON

While it was traditional for the entire extended family to sit together at midnight Mass, Mother, Grandmother, or other willing helpers remained home during the service. After all, there was important work to be done: Cakes needed icing, turkeys needed basting, and tables needed last-minute, festive touches. Those who remained behind knew that the moment the last hymn ended, all in attendance at Mass would rush home for *réveillon,* or "awakening," the family meal that had kept the cooks busy for weeks.

La tourtière, a meat pie, was the highlight of réveillon, but it

For réveillon, New Year's Day, or any special day, French Canadians have always celebrated with family, friends, and food. In another drawing from his series on French-Canadian life, Massicotte shows the "Cake of the Three Kings" dinner that ends the holiday season.

Always eagerly awaited, but never caught making his rounds to French-Canadian homes, Père Noël has long inspired the imagination. This fanciful rendition of the mysterious visitor appeared in an 1862 issue of the Canadian Illustrated News.

cream all had a presence on the dessert table. And one could not forget the doughnuts, fresh from the pillowcases.

Some early French Canadians carried on the European tradition of the Yule log by burning a special birch Christmas log in the fireplace during réveillon. Later, the log was symbolically replaced by the *bûche de Noël*, a chocolate cake shaped like a log and topped with chocolate icing formed into bark-like ridges or a drizzling of white "snow" icing. This special Christmas cake remains a tradition with many Quebec families today.

In the countryside, réveillon was usually served in the farm kitchen. However, any room that could accommodate at least two tables and the 20 to 30 family members in attendance would do. Often adding to their celebration was a fiddler who would play for hours, enticing all takers to show off their square-dancing talents.

With its many courses, multiple tempting desserts, and plenty of good cheer, the réveillon feast often lasted well into the early hours of the morning.

Traditionally, children received a few presents from their relatives during the réveillon celebration. And their stockings often would be filled with oranges, nuts, and little candies from *Père Noël*. However, the true gift giving by custom was reserved for New Year's Day.

Christmas Day itself was a time of relaxation for the adults and games and outdoor sports

always had plenty of company. Other meat dishes included *ragoût de boulettes*, a meat ball and pork hocks stew; minced pork pie; partridge with cabbage; and a goose or turkey. *Les cretons*, a traditional Quebec pork spread, was truly a must. Side dishes included oyster or pea soup, a variety of homemade cheese sauces, head cheese, homemade ketchups, sweet pickles and relishes, chutney, and cranberry sauce.

To top off this traditional meal, at least four or five desserts were served. A variety of pastries and candies, bread pudding, corn meal cake, fruitcakes, sugar pie, maple syrup tarts, and ice for the children. The activities were often followed by a small family dinner in the evening.

NEW YEAR'S DAY

For French Canadians, New Year's Day has always been a time for gathering with family and friends. While réveillon was traditionally a family-only celebration, New Year's Day was the time to throw open the doors and welcome in friends and neighbors alike.

On this, the first day of the year, every child asked for his or her father's blessing. Grown children living far away would return for this important event and the entire family would come together to receive the patriarch's blessing for the year.

Following a morning church service, holiday fare filled the tables for visitors who came calling to exchange best wishes for the New Year. By evening, friends and family would join together in singing, dancing, and other entertainment.

New Year's Day was also the day gifts were exchanged, and children received their presents—at long last—from the Infant Jesus or Père Noël in alternating years.

For French Canadians, New Year's Day has always been a special occasion for traveling from one farm to another in the countryside, or simply stepping next door on narrow streets such as this in Quebec City, to exchange best wishes for the coming year with neighbors and friends.

QUEBEC'S CHRISTMAS TODAY

When France lost the Quebec region to England in 1763, about 65,000 French colonists resided there. Today, there are approximately 8 million Canadians with French ancestry. French Canadians comprise more than 80 percent of the population of the province of Quebec, which prides itself on its French flavor. French is the official language of the province, and Quebec's citizens proudly preserve their uniquely French-Canadian culture.

It is no surprise, then, that French Canadians continue to observe their centuries-old Christmas traditions, adding a pinch of modern flavor here and there. Midnight Mass is still the spiritual heart of Christmas, and réveillon is nearly unchanged. Naturally, some families have chosen to add a few "nouvelle cuisine" dishes to their menus.

A family in Montreal may attend midnight Mass at the world-famous St. Joseph's Oratory, which houses a collection of Nativity scenes from around the world. Or they may celebrate the

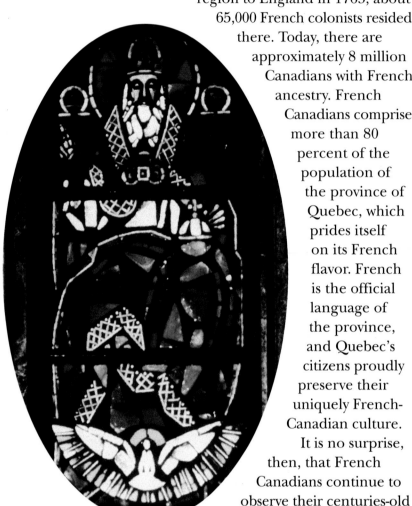

Near Quebec City stands Ste.-Anne-de-Beaupré, a popular place of worship during the Christmas season. This remarkable structure contains 240 stained-glass windows, including this one representing the Eternal Father.

Christ child's birth in Old Montreal at Notre-Dame Basilica. Here, they listen to beloved Christmas hymns and carols played on the 5,772-pipe organ, while taking in its monumental altar and exquisite woodcarvings.

Before attending church services on Christmas Eve and Christmas Day, many city dwellers celebrate with sleigh-riding, cross-country skiing, and ice-skating parties in Montreal's Mount Royal Park. Located in the heart of the city, the park offers miles of snowy trails through groves of tall maple and oak trees, its own 769-foot (234-meter) mountain, and picturesque Beaver Lake. There is no more perfect site for outdoor winter fun.

Some Quebec City residents make the short trip up the river to Ste.-Anne-de-Beaupré to celebrate Christ's birth in the most-visited basilica in North America. With its striking Gallic and Romanesque architecture and its 240 stained-glass windows, Ste.-Anne's is a beautiful setting in which to celebrate this holy season. Nearby is Mont Ste.-Anne. Offering cross-country trails and day and night downhill runs, Mont Ste.-Anne is the most popular winter sports center in the area.

Christmas collections for the poor are very much a part of the French-Canadian tradition. In smaller towns in the Quebec countryside, young people may be heard singing as they travel from door to door requesting donations of food and money for the poor. In cities such as Montreal, churches, businesses, and nonprofit organizations take on the work of soliciting donations for those in need. Churches are a focal point for charitable donations, while food banks and other year-round services step up their efforts at this traditional time of giving.

While some French-Canadian families still save gift giving for New Year's Day, most children look for filled stockings and presents under the tree after réveillon or on Christmas morning. Some lucky French-Canadian children receive presents on Christmas and New Year's Day.

The first day of the New Year continues to be a very special day of celebration for French Canadian families. It is still customary for children to seek the blessing of the head of the family—their grandfather, father, or oldest brother—as the New Year begins. Even now, when many grown children have moved far away from their families, many of them journey home for this important occasion. One week after réveillon, French Canadians sit down for a lavish turkey dinner, either with family members or with friends, and spend the day visiting as they welcome in the New Year.

In Quebec, where a white Christmas is practically guaranteed, the Christmas holidays are an opportunity for outdoor fun. Here, skiers enjoy winter recreation at Quebec's Sugar Loaf Mountain.

CHRISTMAS ACADIAN STYLE

Along New Brunswick's Northumberland Strait, midnight Mass, réveillon, and many other French Christmas traditions light up the season for another group of French-speaking Canadians—the Acadians.

In the early 1600's, France established the colony of Acadia in what are now Nova Scotia, southern New Brunswick, and Prince Edward Island. When the British came to govern the land 100 years later, France abandoned the colony and the people who resided there. In 1755, the British burned their settlements and drove the Acadians from their land.

Scattered in exile, the former French settlers yearned to reclaim the Canadian land they now considered home. In a few years, they began to return. Descendants of the original colonists arrived in strength in the late 1800's, settling in eastern New Brunswick, Nova Scotia, and on Prince Edward Island.

Today, after nearly four centuries, the Acadians continue to be a strong cultural force in Canada's Maritime Provinces. They comprise approximately 35 percent of the population of New Brunswick, concentrated along the province's eastern coast. With its permanent mix of English- and French-speaking citizens, New Brunswick is today Canada's only officially bilingual province.

Canada's Acadians in the 1990's celebrate their Christmas traditions with pride. To mark the weeks preceding Christmas, Acadians construct Advent wreaths in the shape of a cross, which are placed at the foot of the altars in churches. Four candles adorn each wreath. The candles are lighted in succession on the Sundays approaching Christmas.

Christmas Eve, with its religious service and réveillon, is in the French tradition. But unique Acadian foods highlight the family feast. "Pot A," or rabbit pie, is the traditional main course for réveillon. Another Acadian favorite likely to be on any holiday table is *pâté à la râpure*, or rappie pie. This hearty dish is made of layered potatoes, meat, and onions with plenty of bacon, salt, and pepper.

In Acadian communities, the crèche is the dominant Christmas decoration. Inside and outside churches and under the Christmas trees in Acadian homes, the crèche is always present.

The Acadians flew their own flag—a version of the flag of their one-time homeland, France—but with an added yellow star in the upper left corner of the blue stripe.

In place of Santas and snowmen, Acadian families display lighted nativity scenes, often life-size, on their front lawns in celebration of Christmas.

At Christmastime, some Acadian children prepare for their parents a charming, traditional Acadian Christmas gift, the *Bouquet Spirituel.* In years past, young Acadian children, under the guidance of the nuns at school, decorated little cards with dried flowers and colorful drawings. On these cards, each child carefully counted up all the prayers he or she said in the weeks leading up to Christmas. Inspired by the special feelings of the season, and maybe by sibling competition, children often proudly presented their parents with cards marked with hundreds of prayers.

Like French Canadians in Quebec, Acadians celebrate New Year's Day with enthusiasm, sharing a feast with family and friends and greetings of "Happy New Year and Heaven at the end of your days!" with everyone they meet.

Like the Scottish immigrants who also settled in this region of Canada, Acadians traditionally attached significance to the first visitor of the New Year. In Acadian custom, a young boy arriving at the door first on New Year's morning was said to bring good luck in the coming year. In the past, little boys would make the rounds early on the first day of the New Year, knocking on doors and receiving treats. In one village in Nova Scotia, fathers carved special little

wooden hammers the boys could use on this one occasion to tap on their neighbors' doors.

In Acadian communities on Cape Breton, older boys traditionally made their rounds the night before, rapping the corners of houses with long sticks to "beat the New Year in."

When preparing the *gâteau des rois* for the Feast of the Epiphany, Acadian tradition is to bake in a ring and a piece of silver along with the bean and pea. While the bean and pea determine which "king" and "queen" shall reign over the party, the ring reveals the woman who will be first to marry, and the silver marks one who will be rich. When an unexpected person gets the ring or silver, the merriment truly begins.

Even in Toronto, a city rich in cultural diversity, the influence of Canada's British heritage can be seen everywhere at Christmastime, when British traditions help warm the holiday season. Here, colorful Christmas lights bring a glow to the cold December night at Toronto's Nathan Phillips Square and Old City Hall.

THE BRITISH
TRADITION

■

he British were the first Europeans to formally stake a claim in Canada, claiming the land for England in 1497. And although immigrants have arrived here over several centuries, Canada remains first and foremost British in its traditions and customs. Today, about 45 percent of Canadians have some British ancestry, and never is the British influence in Canada more apparent than at Christmas, when plum pudding, fruitcake, evergreen swags and wreaths, caroling,

and many other traditions of early English and Irish settlers abound. At New Year's, descendants of the early Scottish settlers make their mark with Hogmanay.

The season begins on the last Sunday before Advent. Also called "Stir-Up Sunday," this late November day is traditionally spent mixing up batches of English plum pudding. Drenched in flaming brandy, or with tasty

hard sauce or rum sauce dripping down its sides, plum pudding was a must at Christmas for Canada's first British settlers. And today it still tops off a hearty Canadian Christmas dinner.

But plum pudding is just one of the festive Christmas traditions for British Canadians. The season is a time of parties and dances, visits with relatives and friends, and great feasting.

CHRISTMASES PAST

Canadians of all heritages take pride in their country's long-standing ties to Great Britain and hold dear the British traditions of the early settlers. Every year at Christmastime, living history museums and historical homes across the country bring to life the glory of Christmases past for the enjoyment and education of new generations of Canadians.

In almost every city in Canada, the traditions of Christmas are presented in special holiday exhibits at the city's historical homes. To appreciate Canadian Christmas in the British tradition today, one need only see Christmas Past come to life at these living museums.

At living history museums across the country, Canadians today re-create Christmas traditions of the past. At Black Creek Pioneer Village near Toronto, a woman in period costume adds the final touches to a hearth decoration of evergreens and dried flowers.

A BLACK CREEK PIONEER CHRISTMAS

The first settlers in Canada arrived with their hearts and heads full of centuries-old English Christmas traditions. But there was little in their new surroundings to make such a Christmas a reality. As pioneers in the cold, challenging winters of Canada, these colonists often struggled to merely survive and had little time or resources left for celebration. Still, this adversity could not keep Christmas from coming, and these new Canadians established their own ways of celebrating.

Today, visitors to Black Creek Pioneer Village near Toronto can witness Old World Christmas traditions that were given a New World twist. Curators here carefully re-create an early 1800's Canadian Christmas as celebrated by English, Irish, Scottish, and Pennsylvania German settlers in the area.

To replace the dear old holly and mistletoe back home, the English settlers collected wintergreen, hemlock, cedar, and spruce from the woods around them. They twisted evergreen boughs into wreaths, then draped them over mantels and tucked them above pictures. They added native high-bush cranberries, mountain ash, or strings of coral beads to the greenery for a splash of color. A fortunate family might set out a centerpiece bowl of fruits and nuts or add colorful ribbons and white tallow candles to their greenery here and there.

Before the mid-1800's, there was no Christmas tree in a British settler's home. There might be, however, a kissing bough. Hung in a hallway or doorway, the kissing bough—also called a kissing bunch or kissing ball—consisted of a globe or ring made of evergreen boughs and decorated with candles, apples, and nuts.

A lovely pre-Christian symbol of the return of light and life to the world following the winter solstice, the kissing bough earned its name by providing the opportunity for free kisses to any gentleman catching a miss under its influence.

In Anglican churches, sprigs of cedar might be tucked into gimlet holes in the pews. Seasonal greenery decorated the altar, and festive banners proclaiming Christ's birth were often hung on the walls.

For the early Irish settlers, Christmas was considered primarily a religious holiday. Simple home decorations might have included a small, handmade Nativity scene and candles glowing in the window to symbolize the arrival of the Christ child.

THE VICTORIAN CELEBRATION

By the Victorian era, Christmas had grown into a glittering season of celebration in Canada, just as it had in England. The latter part of the 1800's found Canadian cities aglow with dinner parties, dances, christenings, engagement celebrations, and weddings during the Christmas season.

Today, at Mackenzie House, one of Toronto's historical homes representative of the Victorian era, visitors can step back into an 1860 Canadian Christmas. Home to William Lyon Mackenzie, a printer, news-

The traditions that brought Christmas to life for families in the past are re-created at the homes in Black Creek Pioneer Village. Here, children in an Irish Catholic settlers' home set up a crèche, the main focus of this family's modest celebration.

Before there was a Christmas tree in Canada, there was a kissing bough, a sphere of evergreens hung in the home. Like mistletoe, which was added to it later, the kissing bough granted a kiss to couples caught under its spell.

Though gift-giving was still not a major focus for Christmas, advertisements for "store-bought" gifts first appeared in Canadian newspapers in the 1830's and 1840's, and manufactured presents began to become part of the family gift exchange. Books, puzzles, and skates for the children and jewelry and furs for the women shared the spotlight with handmade handkerchiefs and lace doilies, potpourri sachets, doll clothes, and the ever-practical knitted gloves and socks.

On Christmas Eve, once the children were safely tucked into their beds, the presents were placed unwrapped on a table in the parlor.

On Christmas morning, presents were exchanged in a parlor warmed by the light of many candles and a crackling fire. After church came the marvelous midday Christmas feast.

paper publisher, first mayor of Toronto, and an Upper Canadian reformer, this cozy and charming middle-class residence beamed with Christmas cheer. Branches of cedar and pine, decorated with red ribbons, popcorn chains, paper roses, and seasonal mottoes, were draped over the mantels and framed the doorways. The kissing bough, which in the mid-1800's was soon to be replaced by the Christmas tree in nearly every home, was in its final glory.

BOXING DAY

Celebrated the day after Christmas, Boxing Day is one English custom that, while it never reached the United States, has since early times been an important "day off" in Canada.

Historically, Boxing Day in England was the day tradesmen and delivery boys could hope to receive a gratuity from those they served throughout the year. Tradesmen would carry a small "Christmas box" to receive money as they made their rounds on this day.

Boxing Day also became a day for well-to-do families to "box up" clothing and goods to give to servants and the less fortunate. Hence the holiday acquired a second meaning for its name.

Today, Boxing Day continues to be a national holiday in Canada. Now, however, its main significance is as a day of sales at the stores. It is a time to exchange gifts and buy items left waiting on your own Christmas list.

by Sir Henry Cole, who commissioned the design and printing of 1,000 lithographed, hand-colored cards for his friends and acquaintances. Louis Prang brought the custom to North America in the 1860's when he designed chromolithographed cards for sale in the United States.

In 1876, when J. T. Henderson of Montreal offered the people of Canada cards depicting

VICTORIAN CUSTOMS WITH CANADIAN FLAIR

For Canadians in Victorian times, Christmas was a time for getting in touch with loved ones. It was also a season of elaborate decoration. Christmas cards, with their cheery and elegantly colored greetings, became an important tradition the moment they appeared. The first Christmas card was sent in England in 1843

Christmas, a popular custom had its start. Cards featured traditional holiday visions such as rosy-cheeked children riding in a sleigh or skating on a frozen pond, Santa Claus arriving on snowshoes, Indians playing lacrosse, a hostess serving up her delicious steaming plum pudding, and robins flittering about in the snowy woods. Here was a perfect way to send Christmas greetings to friends in

The new Canadians were proud of their country and eager to present its charm to loved ones left behind. These post cards from the Prince Edward Island Museum, dated 1901 (left) and 1905, show the senders' love for Canada and continuing loyalty to Great Britain.

Canada and give relatives back in Great Britain a look at this winter wonderland.

From the country's early days to the present, Canadians have enlivened the Christmas season with song. Hearty caroling from house to house at Christmastime is one cherished English custom that easily made the trip to the New World.

The modern practice of raising money for charities at Christmas is rooted in the late 1800's. Like their French-Canadian neighbors, these Victorians gave an extra push to their efforts on behalf of the needy during the holiday season. Caroling groups then, as now, sought donations for charity—and a little refreshment for themselves as a reward.

SPADINA

Another of Toronto's historical homes is called Spadina. It is here that a 1901 Edwardian Christmas is on display. Spadina was home to four generations of the prominent Austin family, and it was the perfect setting for a sumptuous, extravagant turn-of-the-century celebration.

A long, bell-jingling sleigh ride from the city limits, the Spadina mansion was gloriously decorated in preparation for the rounds of visits and parties expected for the season ahead. Fresh cedar in ropes and wreaths was found everywhere—along the staircase, over doorways, on fireplace mantels. Christmas cards from family and friends overflowed on the billiard table for all to enjoy. Bountiful pots of poinsettias brightened the palm room. And, much to the delight of the children, a red ribbon was tied to the moose's antlers in the back hall.

In 1901, Christmas was for the pleasure of children. Under the influence of Queen Victoria, a doting mother herself, the English-speaking world had taken a new interest in children and their welfare. At no time was the change more apparent than at Christmas. The adult social whirl of parties and dinners and visits continued, but now attention

By 1901, little ones from well-to-do Canadian families could hope to find fancy tea sets, finely dressed porcelain dolls, and such modern factory-made marvels as a perfect miniature stove or sewing machine under the tree.

was focused on the bright little faces that gazed up at the Christmas tree—and the tree was truly a wonder to behold.

With decorations and tree in place, Spadina was readied for a "juvenile party" for the friends of the Austins' two small daughters. Like the adults in Toronto's prominent families, the younger set celebrated the season in style, with an elegant party that included a lavish tea, all manner of treats, and gifts for the children. Even Santa Claus himself was an invited guest.

Children also joined their parents in going to see plays and musical recitals during the holiday season. At home, whole families would share the joy of such games as blindman's buff, twenty questions, and various board games.

CHRISTMAS AND EATON'S

On an early December day in 1905, these same children doubtless would have jockeyed for position on the streets of downtown Toronto to watch the city's first Santa Claus Parade. Arriving at Union Station, Santa rode through the downtown area on a painted packing crate set on a horse-drawn wagon.

One lifetime resident of Prince Edward Island recalls:

"I remember very vividly a Christmas when I was 8 or 9.

There had been a week of very bad storms and by noon

of the day before Christmas, we had had no mail for

about a week, and no parcels from Montreal! Dad

hitched Old Mack, a great strong black horse, to a sleigh

and allowed me to come. We broke the road open to

Victoria, but the mail had not arrived there....We broke

the road open from Victoria to the next town and, again,

no sign of Mr. Walton (the mail carrier) until almost

dark. Then, with a great flurry of sleigh bells and blow-

ing snow, and people rushing about, Mr. Walton and

a week's supply of Christmas mail arrived."

Sponsored for many years by Eaton's department store, the parade continues today under the guidance of a nonprofit organization backed by multiple corporate sponsors. From the early days, when Santa rode alone through the city streets, to today, when 24 colorful floats, an array of marching bands, celebrity clowns, and more travel the parade route, the Santa Claus Parade has remained a Canadian institution.

The name *Eaton* has been associated with Christmas in Toronto and across Canada since the turn of the century. In 1896, the T. Eaton Company issued its first holiday catalog, *Hints for Holiday Gifts.* The catalog was quickly expanded for the next year, offering all sorts of items for adults and children. In the years to come, Eaton's' reach extended far beyond the comfortable city dwellers who enjoyed its parade. Families living in the countryside of the Maritime Provinces far from big cities and stores relied on the Eaton Company—and the mail service—to deliver Christmas to their doorsteps. When a snowstorm in the days before Christmas stopped the mail service, parents and children alike grew anxious.

CHRISTMAS PRESENT

The Santa Claus Parade in Toronto continues today, bigger than ever after almost 90 years. Other cities across Canada now also sponsor Christmas parades, along with many other wonderful public celebrations of the season.

On a Christmas day in the 1990's, Canadian families gather around the television to watch the queen's annual message to the Commonwealth. As they watch, they are bound to snack on fruitcake and Christmas cookies and enjoy cups of hot mulled cider, eggnog, or a dip from the wassail bowl.

MARITIMES CELEBRATIONS

In the quiet countryside and isolated shoreline communities of the Maritime Provinces, children and family life have always been at the heart of Christmas.

On Prince Edward Island, Canada's smallest province, Christmas today as in the past is a quiet church and family holiday. For islanders, life centers around the lovingly restored St. Anne's Catholic Church,

St. Peter's Anglican Cathedral, or one of the many smaller churches that grace the island. Traditionally, even the presents given to the children have some religious significance. A common children's gift, past and present, is a wooden Noah's ark and animals set.

For many people around the world, the mention of Prince Edward Island at Christmas turns their thinking to one young girl's celebration in particular,

Today, age-old British Christmas customs are cherished. British-Canadian families still enjoy a grand Christmas dinner, topped off with the much-loved plum pudding, and when they raise a glass of holiday cheer, it is sure to be filled with eggnog, hot cider, or wassail.

On Prince Edward Island is the home of Lucy Maud Montgomery, author of Anne of Green Gables, *and the setting for her story. Anne's vision of a Christmas morning transformed by an overnight snow has touched the imaginations of children around the world.*

for this is the setting for *Anne of Green Gables,* and the home of its author, Lucy Maud Montgomery.

In Chapter 25 of *Anne of Green Gables,* the author sets the scene for a Prince Edward Island Christmas:

"Christmas morning broke on a beautiful white world. It had been a very mild December and people had looked forward to a green Christmas, but just enough snow fell softly in the night to transfigure Avonlea. Anne peeked out from her frosted gable window with delighted eyes. The firs in the Haunted Wood were all feathery and wonderful. The birches and wild cherry trees were outlined in pearl. The plowed fields were stretches of snowy dimples, and there was a crisp tang in the air that was glorious."

On the island today, the school Christmas concert, a much-loved tradition with more than 100 years of history behind it, is the social event of the season. Hundreds of islanders gather each year to hear the children sing, watch a Christmas play, visit with neighbors, sample the fudge sale, buy homemade Christmas crafts, and fill their plates from tables full of traditional Christmas fare.

HOGMANAY: CELEBRATING A NEW BEGINNING

For settlers from Scotland, Christmas Day was an occasion for pious religious observance, but not a day of celebration. Some early Scottish immigrants even considered it a working day until Christmas was declared an official holiday in Canada in 1867.

Scottish settlers didn't mind working while others feasted on Christmas Day. They knew that their day of celebration was close at hand. Hogmanay, the New Year's Eve celebration, was the grand Scottish holiday of the season.

Hogmanay came into being when Christmas festivities were banned at the time of the Reformation. Today, while it may have faded elsewhere, Hogmanay lives on with vigor in Scotland and among Canadians of Scottish descent.

Because the New Year is a time of new beginnings, a Scottish household would prepare for this special night with a top-to-bottom cleaning. Clocks were wound, bedding changed, clothes mended, instruments tuned, and brass polished. Each person also set out to pay back any debts, return anything borrowed, and square herself or himself with the world on the last day of the old year.

A Hogmanay party on New Year's Eve was full of fun and dancing. Friends and family were invited to enjoy a delicious assortment of tasty snacks.

Part of the fun at Hogmanay was the evening's heavy dose of superstitious customs. At the stroke of midnight, doors and windows all over the house were thrown open, pots and pans banged, bells rung, and noisemakers rattled to drive out the evil spirits and bad luck of the old year. Then all was shut up tight to allow good to flourish in the New Year.

A "first-footer," the first person to enter the house after midnight, determined the luck of the house in the year ahead. Good luck came when a dark-haired man was the first-footer. All visitors to a house, and particularly the first-footer, would carry in bread, salt, and coal, which symbolized life, hospitality, and warmth for the household in the year to come.

WHERE MUMMERS ROAM

"Will ye let the Mummers in?" is the hoarse cry in the night of mobs of people dressed in bizarre get-ups, their faces completely covered and their voices disguised.

"Mummers is welcome!" is the only right reply for those inside who jump to their feet and fling open their doors to let the Mummers trample in from the cold.

During the New Year's Eve Hogmanay celebration at historic Gibson House in North York, Ontario, the "first-footer," or first to cross the threshold after midnight, determines the luck of the house in the year ahead.

Such a scene could only take place in the small, isolated communities of Newfoundland, where, since the first settlers arrived, Mummers have roamed abroad during the 12 nights of Christmas, carrying on an ancient English tradition. Following tradition, bands of friends or relatives dress themselves as weirdly as possible from head to toe, often with men disguised in women's clothing and women disguised as fishermen. Sacks or other coverings completely obscure their faces, and hoarse voices and strange accents are used to disguise their normal way of speech. Then the Mummers, or "jannies" as they are also called, travel to friends' and neighbors' houses where they "demand" entrance. Once inside, they sing wildly, dance jigs, play instruments, and act out short plays while the hosts try to guess their identities. Once guessed, a Mummer must reveal his or her face, then take a seat and resume civilized behavior. He or she can then accept a drink of Christmas cheer from the host family.

Derived from an ancient Roman custom of masquerading as a celebration of freedom from law and morality, and brought to Canada by English settlers, mummering has now died out nearly everywhere in the world except Newfoundland. Once banned even there because of the possibility of mischief, mummering seemed about to disappear altogether.

In recent years, however, Newfoundlanders have taken a renewed interest in their unique means of having fun and spreading Christmas cheer. In some communities, the afternoon of January 6 is reserved for "Little Mummers" to make their rounds in daylight, receiving molasses cookies and Christmas candies for their performances.

TWELFTH NIGHT

Like the French Canadians, Canadians of British descent would customarily bring the Christmas season to a close with a dinner party and special cake on January 6, the Feast of the Epiphany. Called Twelfth Night or Little Christmas in the Anglican tradition, the celebration was otherwise very much the same. A bean and a pea baked into the Twelfth Night cake would determine a "king" and "queen" to rule over the evening's festivities.

CHICKEN BONES AND BARLEY TOYS

Combine an incomprehensible name with a delicious candy snack and you have two Christmas musts for anyone who ever lived in the Maritimes of Canada. Chicken Bones and Barley Toys, two treats with very strange names, have meant Christmas to children along Canada's eastern shores for more than 100 years.

Santa has been stuffing Barley Toys—tasty animal-shaped candies, plain or on sticks—into stockings in eastern Canada for about 175 years now. Manufactured today by the Yarmouth Candy Company in Yarmouth, Nova Scotia, which follows seemingly antique traditional methods, Barley Toys are as much a children's Christmas favorite today as they were in the 1800's.

To make these treats, the Yarmouth Candy kitchen first cooks barley candy (made of sugar, glucose, color, and olive oil) in copper pots on top of open propane (formerly coal) stoves. The liquid is poured from dippers into very small old-fashioned molds shaped as chickens, rabbits, and other animals, as well as steam tractors and a Santa atop a chimney. While the candy hardens, lollipop sticks may be added.

The result is a bright red, green, or yellow candy with a clever shape and a satisfying sweet taste. Why the name *Barley*? It probably comes from an old Scottish term from a children's game, meaning "truce" or "quarter."

In 1885, Ganong Brothers Limited in St. Stephen, New Brunswick, made a cinnamon-flavored, pink, hard candy stick, filled it with chocolate, called it a Chicken Bone—and the rest was Christmas magic. Whether it is the color, which is festive and bright; the taste, which is a distinctive combination of two Christmas favorites; or just the name—Chicken Bones—this little candy quickly took hold of Christmas.

Bringing Christmas trees, Advent calendars, gingerbread houses, holiday cakes, cookies, and more, German settlers gave to Canada a wealth of holiday traditions for all to share.

GERMAN SETTLERS BRING CHRISTMAS MAGIC

◼

Like the English and the French, German settlers arrived during Canada's pioneer days. Around the time of the Revolutionary War in America, many German families living in Pennsylvania sought refuge in Canada. Both "Plain Dutch" (from the word *Deutsch*, or German), as the German Amish and Mennonite settlers were called, and German families who did not share the restrictive life style of the former groups fled the States for Canada in great numbers.

Some German settlers who relocated to Canada were Loyalists who preferred to continue living under England's monarchy. Others came looking for more open land, preferring to move north to a partially settled land than to head toward the unknown of the American West.

Today, about 10 percent of Canadian people claim German ancestry. Many live in Ontario, British Columbia, the Prairie Provinces, and Nova Scotia.

The Germans brought their very special brand of Christmas magic. From the Advent calendar to gingerbread houses to the Christmas tree, many traditions dear to Canadians today were introduced by German settlers in the 1700's and 1800's.

THE CHRISTMAS TREE

German immigrants introduced the Christmas tree to Canada, changing forever the way Canadians celebrate the season.

Evergreens were symbols of life and vitality in ancient times, and trees figured prominently in many pre-Christian religious ceremonies in northern Europe and Scandinavia. Still, it was in Germany in the Middle Ages that what was to be the first ancestor of the Christmas tree appeared.

In a German play about Adam and Eve, a fir tree decorated with apples was called a "Paradise Tree." Soon, German families began putting up Paradise Trees in their homes on December 24, the day on which a feast was held to honor Adam and Eve. By the beginning of the 1600's, German families were setting up what we now know as Christmas trees, complete with cookies, sweets, and colorful decorations hanging from the branches.

When they came to Canada, German families brought along this charming Christmas tradition complete with ornaments

Not long after they first glimpsed Christmas trees in their German neighbors' homes, Canadian settlers of every heritage were adding this charming custom to their own Christmas traditions. Today, the tree is a must for nearly every Canadian family celebrating Christmas.

and decorations. Their new neighbors found the tradition to be strange and wonderful. Soon, Canadian families here and there were decorating trees of their own.

The Christmas tree received a real boost when, in 1841, Queen Victoria's German husband, Prince Albert, put one up for his children's delight at Windsor Castle. In 1848, an engraving of the cozy royal family Christmas scene and a detailed description of the delightful decorations on their tree appeared in a London newspaper. Seemingly overnight, the Christmas tree became a new tradition throughout England, Canada, and the United States.

ALL THE TRIMMINGS

After the Germans introduced the Christmas tree to other parts of the world, Germany became the central source for tree trimmings. While the Victorians influenced the Christmas celebration in Canada and elsewhere during the late 1800's, Germany began supplying decorations on a grand scale.

Whimsically shaped glass ornaments were a German Christmas specialty from the 1870's until World War II. Blown into molds in the shapes of animals, fish, Santas, moons, angels, musical instruments, and every other fanciful Christmas symbol, these delicate hand-painted treasures were what affluent Canadians of the time preferred.

After 1880, every tree of well-to-do Canadians also had its share of German glass balls and "Dresdens," gold and silver cardboard ornaments that were die-stamped and hand-painted. Shiny and lightweight, Dresdens were hollow to allow room to hide a surprise treat. These delights could be had for between 2 cents and 40 cents each.

At the same time, German companies were manufacturing silver foil icicles and "angel hair" for trees around the globe.

The Advent wreath is another German tradition that Canadians took to quickly. These wreaths

Even when fancy trimmings and gifts were in short supply, the Christmas spirit was strong. As shown here, early Pennsylvania-German settlers fashioned decorations from straw, scraps of wool, and cookies; made corn-husk dolls; and knitted useful gifts.

While the Victorians influenced the Christmas celebration in Canada and elsewhere during the late 1800's, Germany began supplying decorations on a grand scale.

consist of four candles placed within a circle of braided fir twigs. In a German settler's home, an Advent wreath would be hung from the ceiling and one of the four candles would be lit on each Sunday in Advent. This tradition is now more commonly followed as a part of public celebration in church services than of private celebrations in homes.

Advent calendars, a German Christmas custom, are especially popular in Canada. Traditionally, an Advent calendar shows a pretty winter scene on its front. Hidden behind numbered doors to be opened each day of December before Christmas are small seasonal illustrations or little chocolates or other tiny treats for children. Stores everywhere in Canada display these colorful calendars, and many Canadian families have made this charming German way of counting the days to Christmas their own.

VISITORS . . . SOME NAUGHTY, SOME NICE

In accordance with long-lived tradition, many German-Canadian children receive small treats from Saint Nicholas on his special day, December 6. In this early December visit, Saint Nicholas also may collect the youngsters' wish lists to deliver to Christkindl (the Christ child) in time for Christmas Eve delivery.

The richness of the German Christmas tradition is truly apparent on Christmas Eve, when German-Canadian families await the arrival of a host of varied magical spirits—some naughty, some nice.

According to German tradition, before Santa comes—in one of several forms—children can expect a visit from his unpleasant servant. Called *Knecht Ruprecht* (Servant Rupert) in some traditions and *Belsnickel* in others, this mean man, dressed in dark robes and an ugly mask, carries bells and whips. He arrives first on Christmas Eve to take an accounting of children's behavior.

Stomping into the house, Santa's servant questions children in a gruff voice about whether they've been good or bad. If he's in the mood, he may chase the little ones around the house, shaking his bells and whips. After he exacts promises to be good, the frightening figure scatters candy for the children and leaves to report back to Santa.

While the mean man himself hasn't been seen in Canada for years, there are still a few equally wild, but much merrier, "belsnicklers" about on Christmas Eve and other nights during the holiday season.

Along the south shore of Nova Scotia, an area settled early on by German immigrants, "belsnickling" is a much-loved Christmas tradition. Similar to the Mummers in Newfoundland,

In a German settler's family, every person helped fill the house with Christmas cheer. Today, children at Black Creek Pioneer Village bring history to life as they string popcorn to decorate the tree in a German-Canadian home.

belsnicklers dress up in outrageous costumes, completely concealing their identities, then set out for a night of fun and surprises. Dropping in on neighbors and friends, belsnicklers act up wildly, stomping, singing loudly, playing instruments, ringing bells, dancing crazily, and staging silly acts while their hosts try to guess their identities. When all are unmasked, it is time for a friendly drink or snack, then off to the next stop. In a spirit of fun, not fury, children are warned to be good.

With the threat of Belsnickel past, it is time to await the arrival of one of several wonderful spirits. Depending on where in Germany their ancestors lived and how strictly their family follows tradition, German-Canadian children can expect presents from Christkindl, delivered by an angel messenger; from Kris Kringle, a German Santa whose name is an adaptation of Christkindl; or from an earlier version of Santa, *Weihnachtsmann*—the ancient man of the woods in winter who wears dark, fur-trimmed robes and carries an evergreen tree.

If the family opens presents on Christmas Eve, called *Heiliger Abend*, or Holy Eve, a child is appointed as Christkindl's helper and hands out the gifts.

This night is also the time to enjoy a meal that mixes old-country and Canadian favorites, such as turkey or roast goose, dumplings, red cabbage, and hot cole slaw. Carrot pudding, rather than plum pudding, is usually the dessert of choice for these Canadians. *Lebkuchen*, spicy cakes molded into various shapes; fruit-filled breads called *stollen*; and an array of Christmas cookies, including gingerbread men and hearts, are also traditional German-Canadian Christmas treats. After the meal and presents, traditional carols are sung and the family heads for church.

According to Mennonite tradition, each child would leave out a plate with his or her name on it on Christmas Eve. In the morning, the children would find the plates filled with oranges, nuts, little candies, and sometimes, a toy or "wish."

THE "PLAIN DUTCH" TRADITION

The austere religious beliefs of the Mennonite settlers from Germany did not include a special holiday of celebration to mark either St. Nicholas Day or Christmas Day. However, Santa Claus in his various German and Canadian forms has always had plenty of Mennonite children on his list.

According to Mennonite tradition, each child would leave out a plate with his or her name on it on Christmas Eve. In the morning, the children would find the plates filled with oranges, nuts, little candies, and sometimes, a toy or "wish" (a small treat a child had hoped for).

A playful Mennonite tradition for Epiphany, January 6, held that any girl who looked into a mirror when alone that day would catch a glimpse of the man she would one day marry.

In small farming communities scattered about Saskatchewan, members of another religious sect who immigrated to Canada from Germany hold a quiet, deeply religious observance of Christmas. Among the Hutterites, all work stops for three days at Christmas. Community members spend their time in prayer and contemplation and attend church services twice each day during this period.

On Canada's west coast, magnificent totem poles such as these in British Columbia's Stanley Park offer powerful silent testimony to the cultural richness of Canada's First Nations peoples.

CELEBRATIONS OF FIRST NATIONS PEOPLES*

■

*I*n the centuries between the time that Canada's first inhabitants made the trek across the frozen Bering Strait—as much as 25,000 years ago—and the arrival of Europeans in the late 1400's, aboriginal peoples spread into every part of Canada. Over time, more than 50 separate First Nations languages and a complex spiritual and cultural landscape spread across this vast country.

The centuries-old beliefs and customs of the native peoples are now accorded a special place of respect as the original foundation for Canada's rich and complex cultural heritage. And like most other Canadians, many of these native peoples follow the Christian faith and celebrate Christmas. Some aboriginal peoples, however, adhere strictly to the time-honored spiritual teachings of their forefathers.

According to the most recent figures, there are 598 aboriginal bands who still call Canada home. The total aboriginal population is officially 341,968. But unofficially, the number of direct descendants from these first Canadian cultures is estimated at between 1 million and 2 million.

*In Canada, the preferred term for these peoples is *First Nations peoples* or *aboriginal peoples*, rather than *Native Americans* or *American Indians*.

THE FIRST CANADIANS

Long before Christmas came to North America, the deep Canadian woods, with their bounty of balsam, spruce, and cedar trees and snowy drifts, were warmed in the darkest days of winter by joyful celebration. Aboriginal peoples inhabited the farthest reaches of Canada, imbuing it with rich cultural traditions.

Not long after Columbus arrived in the New World, legions of European fishermen discovered the teeming fishing waters of the eastern shore of North America and began making annual summer visits across the Atlantic. The European ships became such familiar sights that in 1534, when explorer Jacques Cartier first entered Chaleur Bay, he was greeted by aboriginal peoples who presented beaver skins to trade.

The fur trade expanded rapidly, bringing more and more French trappers and traders. When Champlain founded Quebec City in 1608, permanent contact between the aboriginal peoples of Canada and the Europeans was established.

Quick on the heels of Champlain came French Jesuit missionaries. During the late 1600's to the mid-1700's, the Jesuits successfully established a number of Christian villages among the First Nations peoples. With these missionaries, Christmas came to Canada.

Many of the aboriginal peoples converted to Christianity

soon after encountering the European missionaries.

Over time, aboriginal peoples and Europeans intermarried. As cultures blended, even more native peoples adopted the Christian faith.

A SEASON TO REJOICE

For many of Canada's First Nations groups, winter is a tradi-

tional season of feasting and celebration. For those who live in the Subarctic Northwest Territories—collectively known today as the Dene—winter has always been cause to rejoice.

As in the past, winter solstice festivals among the Northwestern First Nations groups feature feasting, singing, dancing, and drumming, along with racing competitions and games of strength, such as wrestling.

The Iroquois traditionally enjoy six to eight festivals throughout the year. By far, the biggest event in the ceremonial year is the eight-day Mid-Winter Festival. In a special ceremony during the festival, tobacco is burned and the Creator is asked for a blessing on the coming

Sharing and gift-giving ceremonies are central to the cultural beliefs of many of Canada's First Nations peoples. The potlatch, shown here, a centuries-old rite of celebration, is a valued tradition today among some native peoples.

The aboriginal peoples' strong spiritual connection to nature has long found expression in festivals of drama, dance, and song, and in beautiful works of art, like this Tsimshian carved and painted wooden bowl shaped like a beaver carrying a stick.

*The term *nations* refers to individual groups or tribes of the First Nations peoples.

year's crops. The weeklong festival concludes with three days reserved for traditional games.

Cree children make the rounds of their relatives' homes on Christmas Eve. At each home, a cloth bag is hung for each child. On Christmas morning, the children return to each home to collect their bags, now filled with toys, gifts, and candy.

The Mohawk and other peoples in the Iroquois nations* mark New Year's Day as a special day for children. On the first morning of the New Year, children visit the homes of all their mothers' relatives, following a tradition called Noya. The youngsters carry bags that are to be filled with apples, candy, and

traditional doughnuts molded in the shape of dolls.

For Pacific Coast tribes, such as the Haida and Kwakiutl, winter celebrations have always been surrounded by feasts, dancing, and drama.

The most famous ceremony of celebration among all the West Coast peoples is the *potlatch*. Derived from the Nootka word *pachitle*, which means "to give," the potlatch is a celebration that combines feasting, dancing, and gift giving. Traditionally given by a tribe, or by the tribe's chief, a potlatch would culminate in the host lavishing his possessions upon his guests. The more the chief or his people gave away, the greater the prestige.

Today, the potlatch continues to be an important community form of celebration and sharing. Potlatches may be held to celebrate a new house, to help a family or village in need, or simply to distribute good fortune among the whole community. Western peoples celebrate potlatches with renewed pride throughout the year and especially at Christmastime.

In the small villages of the few remaining Tlingit-speaking peoples in Canada's Yukon and along the northern coast of British Columbia, the giving of gifts continues as an important symbol of status and as a strong social bond uniting the families in their isolated communities.

Nowhere is this more evident than in a Tlingit village's celebration of Christmas. This holy holiday in most small villages centers around one large all-community party at the village hall or local school gym.

On Christmas Day, everyone gathers before the village tree in the gaily decorated community hall for speeches, storytelling, and Christmas hymns and carols in their native language. And naturally, there is plenty of good food to go around. Santa Claus himself makes an appearance, and laughter fills the air as children receive and distribute gifts.

The Micmac were the first known inhabitants of Nova Scotia. At the Eskasoni Reserve, a devout Christian community of Micmac peoples has thrived since 1610, when Micmac chief Membertou was baptized in the faith by a visiting Jesuit priest.

Today, Micmac Christians decorate their homes with spruce boughs, sing holiday hymns in their proudly preserved tribal language, and whisper special prayers each night of Advent.

The Micmac Christmas observance on Cape Breton combines First Nations tradition and Christian beliefs in a rich celebration of Christmas. It begins with a processional Mass at the Catholic church on Christmas Eve and ends with a traditional Micmac dance.

AN INUIT CHRISTMAS

It seems right that Santa Claus should make the North Pole his home, only a short hike from his neighbors, the Inuit* of Canada's Far North. The Jolly Old Man, with his devotion to the spirit of gift giving and his hearty endurance of extreme cold, would fit right in among these native Canadians.

Missionaries were among the first outsiders to live among the Inuit. In this cold and distant land, these dedicated teachers found a people eager to listen to the word of God.

The colorful Christmas lights decorating this igloo in Iqaluit send a message of Christmas hope into the dark northern night.

*In Canada, the preferred term for these peoples is *Inuit*, rather than *Eskimo*.

51 ~

Christmas in an Inuit village is celebrated in a grand community get-together with feasting and presents for all at a community hall, school, or other central meeting place. Here, young children visit with Santa Claus at the school festivities in Nonook.

those from the surrounding wilderness gather to share the joy of Christmas over dinner. Traditional favorites such as caribou, seal, and raw, frozen char (a type of trout) are served side by side with turkey. Santa makes his appearance, distributing toys to the children.

Events at an Inuit Christmas celebration include time-honored tests of skill—harpoon throwing, whip cracking, wrestling, and igloo building—along with more modern additions, such as rifle shooting and snowmobile racing. Some all-time favorite Inuit games—One-Hand Reach, The Eagle, One-Foot-High Kick, and the Good Woman Contest—have come to national attention through the creation of an annual Northern Games competition.

An Inuit Christmas celebration is not complete without the traditional Drum Dance, performed by an individual or a group according to local custom. The drumdancer rotates the animal-skin drum and hits its rim with a stick while relating a story through song and dance.

As day darkens, the holiday celebration moves inside. Here they listen to village storytellers and join in games that have been played for generations. The most unusual of the indoor sports

Prior to the arrival of the missionaries, the Inuit practiced a form of nature worship, with a shaman serving as intermediary between the human and spirit worlds. Today, though they retain a strong heritage of cultural traditions in their day-to-day life, most Inuit families are devoutly Christian, practicing the Catholic, Anglican, or Evangelical faith.

The Inuit, with their strong Christian faith, fill the weeks of the Christmas season with holiday festivities. Familiar carols are sung in both Inuktitut (the Inuit language) and English at school concerts.

For many communities, a massive feast involving hundreds of people is the focal point of Christmas. Townspeople and is Throat Singing. Here, two women face each other and make guttural and resonant sounds that imitate sounds of the North—the northern lights, the seashore, the wind—by "throwing" sound into each other's open mouth. The first one to laugh or break the rhythm loses the round.

Many Inuit communities reserve Boxing Day, December 26, or New Year's Eve as the time for a *pallaq*. Roughly translated, the Inuktitut word *pallaq* means the charging or the running, as herds of caribou run.

On this special day, following the Inuit tradition, a family with a special reason to celebrate— a son's first slain caribou, the rare shooting of a polar bear, or some other success—shares its good fortune with neighbors. Standing on top of the house, one or more family members throw gifts, clothing, blankets, and handfuls of candy to those gathered below.

Sporting and skills competitions are a must at an Inuit village Christmas celebration. This photo of an igloo-building competition on Baffin Island was taken by moonlight as there is no sunlight so far north at Christmas.

In celebrating Christmas, First Nations peoples brighten the season with a blend of their peoples' ancient traditions of festival and newly learned Christmas customs. At this Inuit Elders Party, everyone joins in construction of a gingerbread Christmas scene.

To welcome the New Year, there is the new Inuit tradition of the midnight snowmobile parade. The deep, dark silence of the Arctic night is for one night joyfully interrupted as hundreds of lighted snowmobiles roar out, blazing a trail across the icy plain. Adding to the noise are joyful shouts and rifle shots that pierce the air.

CHRISTMAS AMONG THE MÉTIS

The Métis are a uniquely Canadian people. Descendants of aboriginal women and colonial fur traders, many of whom were French, these people played an important part in the struggle for recognition of native rights, as well as in the development of Canada's west. In the Prairie Provinces, the Métis developed a life style that combined aboriginal and European ways and traditions.

The Métis have developed their own special celebrations for the holiday season. The Métis celebration begins on Christmas Eve with a huge family reunion and a traditional meal.

Métis men fire their guns into the air to begin the celebration. Family members and friends dressed in their finest clothes exchange gifts. After the meal, there is dancing to fiddle music, singing, and traditional winter games.

THE HURON CHRISTMAS CAROL

In about 1641, Jean de Brébeuf, a Jesuit missionary living and working among the Huron of southern Ontario, created the first Canadian Christmas carol. Writing Huron words and setting them to an old French tune, Brébeuf brought the story of Christ's birth to life for the Huron people through the symbols and figures in their world.

This first Canadian hymn quickly became a part of the Huron oral tradition, and it was sung in celebration until 1649, when raiding Iroquois warriors killed Brébeuf, destroyed the Jesuit mission, and drove the Huron from their land.

In Quebec, where the Huron relocated, the song lived on. Translated into English and French, the Huron Christmas Carol remains very much a part of Canada's Christmas celebration. Schoolchildren learn the song, and Canadians of all ages hold it dear as a uniquely Canadian Christmas song.

The Huron Carol

'Twas in the moon of wintertime when
    all the birds had fled
That mighty Gitchi Manitou sent angel
    choirs instead.
Before their light the stars grew dim,
And wand'ring hunters heard the hymn:

    Chorus:
    Jesus, your King, is born;
    Jesus is born!
    In excelsis gloria!

Within a lodge of broken bark the tender
    Babe was found.
A ragged robe of rabbit skin enwrapped
    His beauty 'round.
And as the hunter braves drew nigh,
The angel's song rang loud and high:

    Chorus

The earliest moon of wintertime is not
    so round and fair
As was the ring of glory on the helpless
    Infant there.
While chiefs from far before Him knelt
With gifts of fox and beaver pelt.

    Chorus

O children of the forest free, O sons of Manitou,
The Holy Child of earth and heav'n is
    born today for you.
Come kneel before the radiant Boy
Who brings you beauty, peace, and joy.

    Chorus

—*Written by Jean de Brébeuf; translated
into English by J. E. Middleton*

When Ukrainian immigrants arrived in Canada, they brought their Eastern Orthodox celebration of Christmas. Here, worshipers at the Ukrainian Cultural Heritage Village near Edmonton gather before an ice cross to celebrate the Feast of Iordan at the end of the Christmas season.

UKRAINIAN CHRISTMAS CUSTOMS

■

hen Ivan Pylypow and Wasyl Eleniak, Canada's first two Ukrainian immigrants, exchanged a hearty *"Khrystos Rodyvsya!"* ("Christ is born!") and *"Slavim Yoho!"* ("Let us glorify Him!") on Christmas Eve, 1891, this North American country became home to another Christmas tradition. This tradition blends deeply religious Eastern Orthodox ceremony with age-old agrarian customs.

Those first Ukrainian immigrants found the farmland they sought in the plains of western Canada, and a mass migration began. Between 1892 and 1894, the first major group of Ukrainians settled near Star-Edna, northeast of Edmonton, Alberta. Several major waves of settlers followed in the coming years.

By 1914, roughly 200,000 Ukrainian immigrants were living in Canada, mostly in Alberta, Manitoba, and Saskatchewan. In the 1920's, another 60,000 arrived. As they turned the vast stretches of Alberta and Saskatchewan into shimmering fields of grain, they made a new home for their religious traditions.

The promise of a new life has continued to attract Ukrainians to Canada. At last count, more than 10 percent of the population of Alberta, Manitoba, and Saskatchewan claimed Ukrainian heritage. Today, these Canadians continue the winter cycle of Christmas traditions that have been passed down for generations.

The religious observance of Christmas in Ukrainian homes begins with the Feast of St. Philip in November. Here, a Ukrainian Canadian sweeps his house in preparation for the celebration to come.

ANCIENT RITES

According to the Julian calendar of the Eastern Orthodox Church, Christmas Eve, or *Sviat Vechir*, and Christmas Day, or *Rizdvo*, arrive for Ukrainians on January 6 and 7; New Year's Day occurs one week later. Ukrainians in Canada today, most of whom follow the Eastern Orthodox Church or the Ukrainian Catholic Church, celebrate their own special Christmas traditions on these days. Some now enjoy two Christmases, joining the countrywide celebration on December 25 as well.

Many Ukrainian Christmas traditions came to life thousands of years ago in the farm villages of Ukraine, where religion, like survival, focused on the success of the harvest. Agrarian symbols whose meanings predate Christianity remain the center of today's Christmas celebration.

While the Ukrainian-Canadian Christmas celebration comes later than that of most other Canadians, the preparations begin earlier. Following the Julian calendar, Ukrainian immigrants at the turn of the century began a ritualistic cleansing of their homes, yards, and barns, along with fasting and purification of the body and soul, on the Feast of St. Philip, or *Pylypiwka*, in November.

SVIATA VECHERA

The heart of Christmas for Ukrainian Canadians is *Sviata Vechera*, or Holy Supper, on Christmas Eve, January 6. A bountiful family meal ends this traditional day of fasting. Once an agricultural celebration, Sviata Vechera is filled with overlapping Christian and agrarian symbols. Twelve dishes are served, representing the most valuable products of the field, garden, and orchard. The 12 dishes also symbolize the 12 apostles, and at the same time represent the 12 cycles of the moon around the earth. The entire meal is meatless and milkless as a sign of respect for the farm animals, because the family relies on them for food, clothing, and transportation all year long.

Before supper can be served, a sheaf of wheat called the *didukh* (meaning "Grandfather," from the Ukrainian word for grandfather, *did*) is carried in by the father or head of the household. He must walk around the interior of the house three times before placing the wheat in a corner of the kitchen or dining room in a position of honor near the family's holy icon. The didukh will remain in place throughout the Christmas season.

Traditionally made up of the best stalks of wheat gathered during *Obzhynky*, the harvest festival in August, the didukh

represents the gathering of all the family—living, dead, and yet to be born. The souls of the family's ancestors are thought to reside in the sheaf of wheat

throughout the holiday celebrations. This all-important Ukrainian symbol stands for both the Christian belief in an afterlife and the bountiful fertility of the land.

In generations past, many Ukrainian farmers would take the didukh outside on January 19. There they would arrange it on the ground in the shape of a cross, then burn it to release the

Pictured here on a Ukrainian Christmas card, the didukh is a sheaf of wheat that represents the family. Because the didukh is said to contain the souls of the family's ancestors, it is placed in a position of honor in the home for the Christmas season.

Today, Ukrainian-Canadian families still celebrate Sviata Vechera, or Holy Supper, with careful attention to every detail. On this present-day Christmas Eve table, the kolach is in its place of honor.

spirits of the dead back into the soil and mark the end of the Christmas season. Others would save the didukh to burn in the orchards in spring to bring strength and health to their trees. Today, urban Ukrainian Canadians may save their didukh from year to year.

To prepare the Sviata Vechera table, a bit of fresh sweet hay is tucked under the white table-cloth and a *rushnyk*, an embroidered runner, is laid on top. The hay is placed in memory of the manger where the Christ child was born. The two table coverings are symbolically spread for

the living and for the dead. More hay is spread out under the table to remember the animals in the stable where Christ was born. This hay is often sprinkled with tiny treats of candy, nuts, and coins for the children to discover. Another tradition is that of placing a clove of garlic at each corner of the table. This is done in an effort to keep illness away from the family. Finally, an extra place is set at the table so that the spirits of departed loved ones can share in the celebration of Christmas Eve.

THE FIRST STAR

While wonderful smells drift from the kitchen, children gather around a window and eagerly watch the night sky. When one of them spots the first star of the evening, thought on this night to be the Star of Bethlehem, the glorious meal can begin.

Before dinner begins, three loaves of Christmas bread, or *kolach*, are placed in the center of the table, usually one on top of the other. Often revered with rituals and prayer, the bread symbolizes the eternity of God and the perpetuance of the family. Placed one atop another, the three loaves stand for the Holy Trinity. A single white beeswax candle is placed in the middle of the top loaf. Lighted, the candle symbolizes Jesus Christ, "The Light of the World." Often, the head of the household would carry a kolach with its lighted

Selecting ancient agrarian songs, traditional Ukrainian carols, or popular English-language carols, Ukrainian Canadians sing at the homes of friends and neighbors on Christmas Day.

candle while blessing his farm and family. He believed that the smoke rising from the candle would carry his prayers to God.

Supper begins with the most significant dish of all, *kutia.* Kutia is a blend of boiled wheat, poppy seeds, and honey—all traditional products of the harvest considered to be favorite foods of the ancient gods. Each ingredient of this first dish has a special significance on Christmas Eve. The wheat symbolizes prosperity, the poppy seeds stand for the beauty of the land, and the honey represents the hope that the family will stick together.

The head of the household makes the rounds of the table, serving kutia to each family member. As each person receives a spoonful, he or she says *"Khrystos Rodyvsya!"* ("Christ is born!"), and the head of the household answers *"Slavim Yoho!"* ("Let us glorify Him!"). When everyone has been served, the host throws a spoonful of kutia at the ceiling. The more kutia that sticks to the ceiling, the better the outlook for prosperity in the coming year.

The next 11 dishes of the Christmas Eve meal may vary slightly from house to house, but all must be meatless and without animal fat, milk, or anything made from milk, for Sviata Vechera is the last night of the 40-day fasting period.

After everyone has indulged to his or her heart's content, the family may linger around the table singing carols until it is time to head to church for midnight Mass.

RIZDVO

Ukrainian Canadians spend Christmas Day, *Rizdvo*, visiting with friends, neighbors, and relatives; singing carols; and enjoying good food and drink. In traditional Ukrainian homes, Santa does not leave presents on the night before Christmas. But Ukrainian children are never overlooked. In fact, these fortunate children are some of the first to receive their Christmas treats each year.

On December 19, St. Nicholas Day according to the Julian calendar, wise Saint Nicholas, dressed in his bishop's robes, visits Ukrainian-Canadian homes. A kind, fair man, Saint Nick gives presents to those children who were good and is rumored to leave twigs or a lump of coal for the not-so-nice. Presents are left under a tree in most Ukrainian-Canadian homes these days, though long ago, Saint Nicholas threw presents for the poor and needy, especially children, through an open window.

Dressed in his bishop's robes, St. Nicholas makes his rounds to Ukrainian-Canadian homes on St. Nicholas Day. Here, the wise old gentleman visits with young admirers and passes out bags of treats.

BLESSING THE WATER

The Ukrainian-Canadian Christmas season ends on January 19, with the *Iordan*, the Feast of Jordan. This day commemorates the baptism of Jesus by John the Baptist in the River Jordan.

Traditionally on Iordan, the water—usually a river, lake, or well—was blessed at the site of a large ice cross constructed by the men of the parish. The ceremony would take place either in the churchyard or at the site where the ice was cut. Parishioners would make a procession to the ceremony carrying banners, the book of the Gospels, *triitsia* (a special three-pronged candlestick), and a processional cross. After the blessing, worshipers would take home water to be used by the parish priests in blessing their families, livestock, and farm buildings, praying that God would keep them from harm in the coming year.

Today, the ceremony of Iordan is a bit different, with priests in the church blessing tubs of

At the Ukrainian Cultural Heritage Village, worshipers participate in the Feast of Iordan ceremony, which closes the Christmas holiday season. Here, priests bless the water which is then taken to bless families, homes, farms, and animals.

At the end of the Christmas season, the didukh is spread into the shape of a cross on the ground and burned. As it burns, children leap through the flames, hoping their ancestors' spirits will not follow or cause them bad luck during the year.

water from which worshipers can take cupfuls to sprinkle on their homes. Still, at the Ukrainian Cultural Heritage Village near Edmonton, Alberta, this important rite is reenacted every year.

Like Christmas, Iordan begins with a Holy Supper the night before. To prepare for Iordan, early settlers made wax candles and crosses from wax and dough to adorn the doors of their homes or used chalk or honey to mark a cross above the doors and windows of their buildings. Again, these rituals provided protection

for the settlers in the new year.

The Eve of Iordan is known as the second *Sviat Vechir* (Holy Evening), sometimes called *Shchedryi Vechir*. Following a one-day fast, this day's meal is also traditionally *shchedryi* (generous), consisting of 12 meatless and milkless dishes. The meal begins with kutia and a prayer for the year to come.

Carrying the didukh to the yard and burning it on Iordan officially marks the end of the Christmas season for Ukrainian Canadians.

KISSING BOUGH

Hang this Christmas decoration in your living room or in a hallway.
Then step back and watch the fun!

MATERIALS

heavy wire, about 4 feet long
evergreen boughs
    (most Christmas tree vendors will
    sell —or give away—their extras),
    4 feet in length all together
two dozen green twist ties

red or green ribbon
12 decorative red apples
    (not edible)
two 18-inch lengths of red,
    green, or gold cord
one bunch of mistletoe

WHAT TO DO

1 Shape the wire into a ring, overlapping and twisting the ends together to hold the shape.

2 Cover the wire ring with the boughs of evergreen. Use the twist ties to hold the boughs in place. Use as many boughs as needed to completely cover the wire.

3 Using the red or green ribbon, tie the decorative apples to the wire every 4 inches so that they hang below around the entire circumference of the circle. (You may hang all the apples the same distance from the kissing bough— about 6 inches—or stagger them.)

4 Tie the ends of the two lengths of cord to the wire so that each end is 12 inches away from the one next to it.

5 Hang the kissing bough by the two cords from a hook in the ceiling. Join the cords at the hook with a twist tie. On the same hook, hang the bunch of mistletoe so that it hangs at least 6 inches lower than the apples on the bough.

STUFFED CANADA GOOSE ORNAMENT

*Allow several days to make this ornament, to be sure
the glue dries completely after each step.*

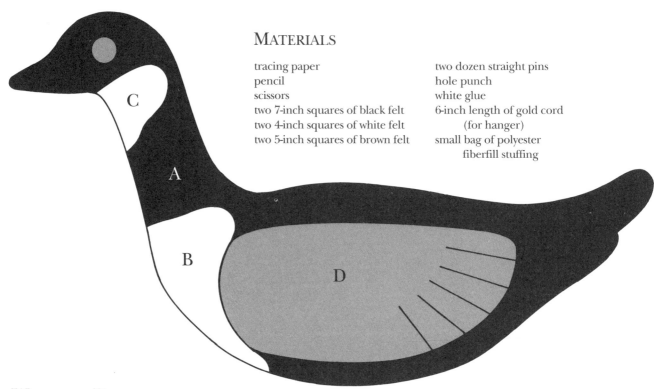

MATERIALS

tracing paper
pencil
scissors
two 7-inch squares of black felt
two 4-inch squares of white felt
two 5-inch squares of brown felt

two dozen straight pins
hole punch
white glue
6-inch length of gold cord
   (for hanger)
small bag of polyester
   fiberfill stuffing

WHAT TO DO

1 Trace patterns A, B, C, and D onto tracing paper. Cut out patterns along the outlines.

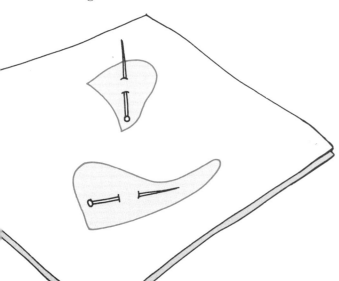

2 Place one 7-inch square of black felt exactly on top of the other. Pin pattern A (the goose's body) onto the center of the two squares, making sure the pattern is pinned to both squares. Carefully cut the felt along the outline of the pattern.

3 Place one 4-inch square of white felt exactly on top of the other. Pin patterns B and C (the white accents) onto the white felt, making sure they are pinned to both squares. Carefully cut the felt along the outlines of the patterns.

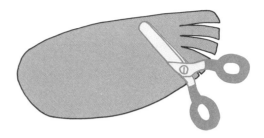

4 Place one 5-inch square of brown felt exactly on top of the other. Pin pattern D (the goose's wing) onto the center of the two squares, making sure the pattern is pinned to both squares. Carefully cut the felt along the outline of the pattern.

5 Using the hole punch, punch out two circles from the remaining brown felt. These will be the goose's eyes.

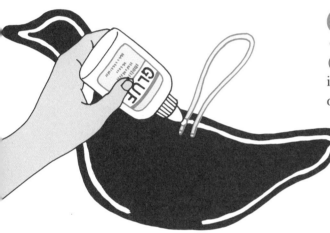

6 Squeeze a small amount of glue along the edges of one side of the goose's body, leaving a 1-inch opening along the underside of the goose, where there should be no glue. Stick the two ends of the gold cord to the glue along the goose's back. Dab a small amount of glue on top of the ends of the cord, as shown in the figure above. Place the other side of the goose's body on top of the glue and cord—matching head to head and tail to tail. Press together. Be sure there is still an opening along the underside of the goose. Glue the goose's eyes to its head. Allow the glue to dry overnight.

7 Cut five to seven ³/₄-inch diagonal slits about ¹/₄ inch apart into the wings (pattern D), as shown in the figure above.

8 Glue the white accents (patterns B and C) onto both sides of the goose, matching the illustration on page 66.

9 Place glue along the edges of the wings that do not have slits. Stick the wings (pattern D) to the goose, matching the illustration on page 66. Allow the glue to dry for a couple of hours.

10 Stuff the polyester fiberfill stuffing into the goose through the opening along its underside, as shown in the illustration below. Use a pencil to get the stuffing into the head and neck and tail areas. Do not overstuff.

11 Glue the opening closed. Allow to dry for at least one hour. The goose is now ready to decorate your tree.

BALSA WOOD
MAPLE LEAF

*Allow two days to make this ornament, to be sure the
shellac and paint dry completely after each step.
Ask an adult to help you cut out and paint the leaf.*

MATERIALS

tracing paper
pencil
scissors
6-inch square of balsa wood
craft knife
12-inch square of heavy cardboard
2 squares of sandpaper—
    one very fine and one with
    a coarser grade

emery board
8-ounce can of clear shellac
¾-inch or 1-inch
    touch-up paintbrush
turpentine
paper towels
8-ounce can of red enamel
thin, sharp nail
4-inch length of white yarn

WHAT TO DO

1 Trace pattern of maple leaf
onto tracing paper. Cut
out pattern along outline.

2 Place pattern in center of balsa wood and carefully trace the outline onto the wood. Remove the pattern and fill in any missing details.

3 Cut out the pattern of the maple leaf with the craft knife. To protect your work surface, place the heavy cardboard square under the wood before cutting.

6 Paint one side of the maple leaf with red enamel, then clean your paintbrush. Allow leaf to dry for one to two hours, then apply a second coat. Clean your brush again. Allow leaf to dry for another one to two hours, then turn it over. Paint and repaint the other side, making sure to paint the edges of the maple leaf as well.

Again, allow to dry for one to two hours after each coat, and clean your brush between coats.

7 To make a hanger for the maple leaf, punch a hole about $1/4$ inch from the top with the nail. String white yarn through the hole and tie the ends together.

4 Smooth the surfaces of the maple leaf with the fine sandpaper. Smooth the edges with the coarser sandpaper. Use the emery board to get into the tight spaces of the leaf's edges.

5 Paint one side of the maple leaf with shellac. Allow shellac to dry for one hour. Turn the leaf over and paint the other side, as well as the edges. Allow to dry for one hour. While leaf is drying, clean your paintbrush in turpentine, then rinse it in water. Pat with paper towels to dry.

CANADIAN RECIPES

OYSTER SOUP

3 tbsp. butter, melted
1 tsp. finely chopped onion
$1\frac{1}{2}$ pints oysters with liquid

$1\frac{1}{2}$ cups milk
$\frac{1}{2}$ cup cream
salt to taste

white pepper to taste
2 tbsp. chopped parsley
2 egg yolks, beaten

In the top pan of a double boiler, melt butter over direct heat. Sauté onion in butter until onion is transparent. Add oysters with liquid, milk, cream, salt, and pepper. Place pan over boiling water in the bottom pan of the double boiler. When the milk becomes hot and the oysters float, remove from heat. In a small bowl, gradually add 2 or 3 tablespoons of hot soup to beaten yolks. After mixing, slowly add eggs to the hot soup. Heat slowly for another minute or so, but do not allow to boil. Serve immediately.

Makes 4 servings.

CIPAILLE (MEAT AND POTATO PIE)
*(Note: Make the 9-inch double-crust pie pastry recipe on page 71 **twice** for use in this recipe.)*

2 lbs. boneless, skinless
　chicken breast
2 lbs. beef tenderloin
2 lbs. pork tenderloin
2 large onions, chopped

2 large potatoes, peeled,
　cut into 1-inch cubes
$\frac{1}{2}$ tsp. salt
pepper to taste
$\frac{1}{4}$ tsp. nutmeg

$\frac{1}{4}$ tsp. cinnamon
$\frac{1}{4}$ tsp. allspice
2 cups chicken or beef stock
pastry for *two* 9-inch double-
　crust pies (page 71)

Cut chicken and meats into 1-inch cubes; place in a large bowl. Mix in onions. Cover and refrigerate overnight.

Preheat oven to 400 °F. In a small bowl, combine spices. Spray the bottom and sides of a 3-quart casserole dish with cooking spray. Divide pastry dough into four equal parts. Roll out each to $\frac{1}{4}$-inch thickness, large enough to line the bottom of the casserole. Line casserole dish with one pastry round. Spoon in one-third of the meat mixture, one-third of the potatoes, and one-third of the spices. Place another pastry round on top of potatoes. Prick pastry with a fork to allow steam to vent. Top pastry with another third of the meat mixture, potatoes, and spices, and another pastry round. Again, prick the pastry with a fork. Repeat layering once more, finishing with pastry. Cut a 1-inch slit in the center of the top pastry.

Pour enough stock through the slit until liquid appears. Cover casserole dish and bake 45 minutes. Reduce oven temperature to 250 °F and continue baking for 6 hours or until top crust is golden-brown.

Makes 8 servings.

MEAT BALL STEW

1 medium onion, chopped
1 clove garlic, minced
2 tbsp. butter, melted

1 lb. ground pork
1 tsp. ground ginger
1 tsp. ground cloves

2 tbsp. olive oil
3 cups beef stock
1 tbsp. flour

Sauté onion and garlic in butter until onion is transparent. In a medium bowl, mix together pork, ginger, cloves, and onion and garlic mixture. Shape meat into 2-inch balls. In a large skillet, brown meat balls in olive oil over medium heat.

Add beef stock and simmer 30 minutes. Blend flour with a small amount of water. Add flour mixture to beef stock, stirring constantly until sauce thickens.

Makes 8 servings.

CANDIED CRANBERRIES

$2\frac{1}{2}$ cups sugar
$1\frac{1}{2}$ cups water
1 quart cranberries

In a medium saucepan, stir sugar in water over medium-high heat. Bring mixture to a boil, stirring constantly. Pour the boiling mixture over the cranberries in a large heat-resistant bowl. Place bowl in a steamer 45 minutes. Remove bowl and cool cranberries without stirring. Set in a warm,

dry place 3 to 4 days. When the syrup has a jellylike consistency, remove cranberries and allow to dry 3 days longer. Turn cranberries often so they will dry completely. When they can be handled easily, store in a tightly covered container.

Makes about 1 quart.

PASTRY FOR 9-INCH DOUBLE-CRUST PIE
(for Cipaille, Tourtiere, or Mincemeat Pie)

$2\frac{1}{2}$ cups flour
dash salt
$\frac{1}{2}$ cup butter

$\frac{1}{2}$ cup shortening
6-8 tbsp. water

In a large mixing bowl, combine flour and salt. Cut in butter and shortening using a pastry knife until the largest pieces of the mixture are about the size of a pea. Sprinkle water over the mixture, one tablespoon at a time. Use a fork to gently distribute the water, until a soft dough forms. Gather the dough into a ball. Separate into two equal balls. Refrigerate for about an hour.

Remove one ball of dough from refrigerator and place on a lightly floured surface. Press ball with palm of hand to flatten slightly. With floured rolling pin, roll from center to edges until crust is $\frac{1}{8}$-inch thick. Repeat process with the other ball.

Makes dough for a 9-inch double crust.

FRUIT FOOL

½ cup sweetened whipping cream
1 cup unsweetened applesauce or
    other fruit purée
¼ tsp. almond extract

Whip cream until stiff. Fold in fruit purée and almond extract. Chill mixture in refrigerator. Serve with fresh fruit or shortcake.
    Makes 4 servings.

MULLED CIDER

1 quart apple cider
4 or 5 whole cloves
cinnamon stick

In a medium saucepan, mix together ingredients over medium heat; heat well, but do not allow to boil.
    Makes 4 servings.

HONEY CAKE

1 cup honey
½ cup butter
1 cup brown sugar
4 eggs, separated
1 tsp. vanilla

3 cups flour
1½ tsp. baking soda
1 tsp. baking powder
½ tsp. cinnamon

½ tsp. ginger
¼ tsp. salt
½ cup cooled strong coffee
½ cup walnuts, chopped

Preheat oven to 325 °F. In a small saucepan, bring honey to a boil; allow to cool to room temperature. In a large bowl, cream butter and brown sugar. Beat in egg yolks, one at a time. Add cooled honey and vanilla.

In a separate bowl, sift together flour, baking soda, baking powder, cinnamon, ginger, and salt. Blend dry ingredients into butter mixture, alternately with coffee.

Stir in nuts. Beat egg whites until stiff but not dry; fold into batter. Pour batter into a well-greased loaf pan. Bake for 1 hour. Cool on rack 10 minutes. Remove from pan. Once cooled, wrap in plastic wrap to keep moist. Stored in a cool place, this cake will improve with age.
    Makes 10 to 12 servings.

HARD SAUCE *(for English Steamed Plum Pudding)*

1 cup sifted powdered sugar
½ cup butter
1 tsp. vanilla
dash salt

Gradually add sugar to butter. Beat until well blended and fluffy. Add vanilla and salt. When sauce is smooth, chill thoroughly.

FRUITCAKE

1 cup butter	2 cups flour	$\frac{1}{2}$ cup *each* figs, dates,
1 cup brown sugar	1$\frac{1}{2}$ tsp. baking powder	and pitted prunes, chopped
4 eggs	2 cups raisins	$\frac{1}{2}$ cup candied cherries, sliced
2 tsp. vanilla	1 cup currants	1 cup walnuts, chopped
1 tsp. nutmeg	$\frac{1}{2}$ cup *each* candied orange	1 cup apple cider
1 tsp. cinnamon	and lemon peel, chopped	

Preheat oven to 275 °F. In a large mixing bowl, cream together butter and brown sugar. Add eggs, one at a time, beating well after each addition. Add vanilla, nutmeg, and cinnamon. Set aside.

In a separate bowl, sift together flour and baking powder. Set aside.

In another bowl, mix together all the fruits and nuts. Add 1 cup flour mixture.

Stir into butter mixture. Gradually add remaining flour, alternating with apple cider.

Pour batter into two loaf pans that have been well-greased, lined with brown paper, and greased again. Bake about 2 hours or until toothpick comes out clean. Cool on rack 10 minutes. Remove from pan.

Makes 2 dozen servings.

MINCEMEAT

(Note: Make this recipe two weeks before you plan to serve it.)

4 cups finely chopped peeled apples	$\frac{1}{4}$ tsp. ground cloves	3 lemons, grated rind and juice
4 cups raisins	1 tsp. nutmeg	1 cup apple juice
$\frac{1}{2}$ cup citron, chopped	$\frac{1}{4}$ tsp. salt	$\frac{1}{4}$ cup brandy (optional)
2 tsp. cinnamon	3 cups brown sugar	

In a large saucepan, combine apples, raisins, citron, spices, salt, brown sugar, lemon juice and rind, and apple juice. Bring to a boil. Reduce heat and simmer 1$\frac{1}{2}$ hours, stirring frequently.

Remove mixture from heat; add brandy, if desired. Spoon into hot sterilized canning jars. Process in boiling-water bath for 15 minutes. Mincemeat will be ready for use in about 2 weeks.

Makes about 7 cups.

For Mincemeat Pie: Preheat oven to 425 °F. For each double-crust, 9-inch pie (page 71), mix 2 cups mincemeat with 2 cups chopped apple. Spoon into prepared pie shell; top with pastry and seal edges. Prick top crust with fork to vent. Bake for 15 minutes; reduce heat to 350 °F and bake for 30 minutes more or until pastry is lightly browned.

Sugar Pie

pastry for 9-inch single-crust pie (below)

1 1/2 cups brown sugar
3/4 cup whipping cream

8 tsp. cornstarch

Preheat oven to 425 °F. Line pie pan with pastry. In a medium bowl, mix together brown sugar, whipping cream, and cornstarch. Pour mixture into prepared pie shell. Bake 10 minutes, then lower temperature to 325 °F and continue baking for 30 minutes or until filling is set and golden.

Makes 6 servings.

Maple Syrup Pie

pastry for 9-inch single-crust pie (below)
1/4 cup flour

1/2 cup water
1 cup maple syrup
1 egg, slightly beaten

2 tbsp. butter
whipped cream

Preheat oven to 450 °F. Line 9-inch pie pan with pastry; prick several times with a fork. Bake pie shell for 10 minutes or until lightly browned. Allow pie shell to cool. Mix flour and water until smooth.

In a medium saucepan, stir together flour mixture and maple syrup. Stir in egg. Cook over medium heat, stirring constantly, until thick. Add butter and stir until melted.

Pour mixture into cooled pie shell. Allow pie to cool at room temperature until set. Serve topped with whipped cream.

Makes 8 servings.

Pastry for 9-inch Single-Crust Pie (for Sugar Pie or Maple Syrup Pie)

1 1/2 cups sifted all-purpose flour

1/2 tsp. salt
1/2 cup butter

4 to 5 tbsp. very cold water

Sift flour and salt into a medium mixing bowl. Using two knives, cut in butter until pieces are the size of small peas. Sprinkle 1 tbsp. water over contents of bowl; toss gently with fork to mix. Repeat this step until all water has been added. Form mixture into a ball; place on lightly floured surface. Press ball with palm of hand to flatten slightly. With floured rolling pin, roll from center to edges until crust is 1/8-inch thick.

MOLASSES TAFFY

1 cup sugar
1 cup brown sugar
2 cups molasses
1 cup light corn syrup
1 cup water
¼ cup butter

In a large saucepan, mix together sugars, molasses, corn syrup, and water. Cook over medium heat, stirring constantly, until temperature on a candy thermometer reaches just below the soft crack stage (268 °F) or until sugar is dissolved.

Continue cooking, stirring occasionally, until a small amount of mixture threads when dropped into cold water. Remove from heat and stir in butter. Pour slowly onto a buttered slab or buttered cookie sheet on a cooling rack. Allow to cool slightly, then pull with your fingertips, allowing a spread of about 18 inches between your hands. Fold mixture back on itself. Repeat this motion rhythmically until the mixture forms a glistening ribbon and the ridges on the twist begin to hold their shape. Roll mixture into long, thin strips. Cut into pieces and place on buttered wax paper.

Makes about 2 pounds.

CANADIAN DOUGHNUTS

3 cups flour
¾ cup sugar
3 tsp. baking powder
1 tsp. baking soda
½ tsp. nutmeg
½ tsp. cinnamon
¼ tsp. salt
½ cup buttermilk
3 tbsp. butter, melted
2 eggs, slightly beaten
vegetable oil for frying
cinnamon-sugar mixture
  (1 part cinnamon to
  4 parts sugar)
powdered sugar

Mix together flour, sugar, baking powder, baking soda, nutmeg, cinnamon, and salt; set aside. Blend buttermilk and butter into eggs; gradually add dry ingredients to make a soft dough. Chill in refrigerator 2 to 3 hours.

On floured board, roll dough to ¼-inch thickness. Using a floured doughnut cutter, cut out doughnuts. Cook in hot oil for 1 to 2 minutes per side or until golden brown. Drain on paper towels. Roll warm doughnuts in a cinnamon-sugar mixture or powdered sugar, if desired.

Makes about 1½ dozen doughnuts.

WHENCE ART THOU, MY MAIDEN?

D'où Viens-Tu, Bergère?

TRANSLATION: WILLIAM MCLENNAN, 1866

TRADITIONAL FRENCH CANADIAN

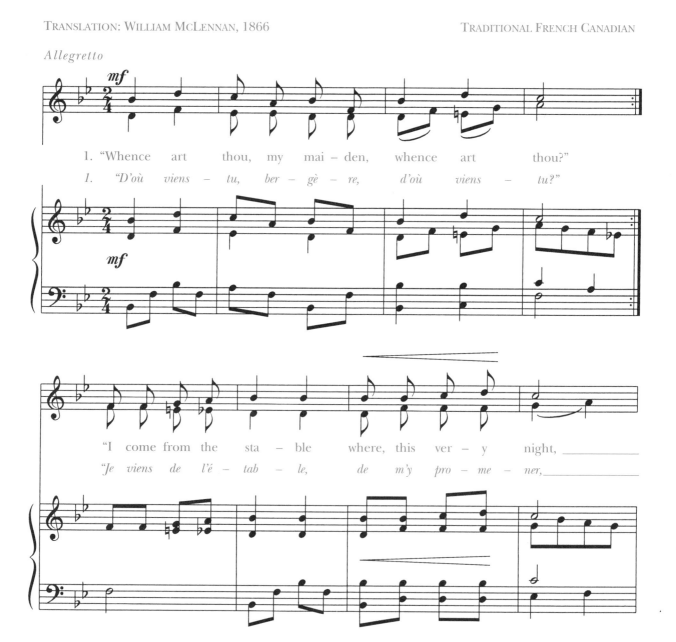

1. "Whence art thou, my mai-den, whence art thou?"
1. "D'où viens-tu, ber-gè-re, d'où viens-tu?"

"I come from the sta-ble where, this ver-y night,_____
"Je viens de l'é-tab-le, de m'y pro-me-ner,_____

I, a shep–herd maid – en, saw a won – drous__sight."

J'ai vu un mi–ra – cle ce soir ar – ri – vé."

2. "What saw'st thou, my maiden,
    what saw'st thou?
   What saw'st thou, my maiden,
    what saw'st thou?"
   "There within a manger,
    a little Child I saw
   Lying, softly sleeping,
    on a bed of straw."

3. "Nothing more, my maiden,
    nothing more?
   Nothing more, my maiden,
    nothing more?"
   "There I saw the mother
    her sweet Baby hold,
   And the father, Joseph,
    trembling with the cold."

4. "Nothing more, my maiden,
    nothing more?
   Nothing more, my maiden,
    nothing more?"
   "I saw ass and oxen,
    kneeling meek and mild,
   With their gentle breathing
    warm the holy Child."

5. "Nothing more, my maiden,
    nothing more?
   Nothing more, my maiden,
    nothing more?"
   "There were three bright angels
    come down from the sky,
   Singing forth sweet praises
    to our God on high."

2. *"Qu'as-tu vu, bergère,*
    qu'as-tu vu?
   Qu'as-tu vu, bergère,
    qu'as-tu vu?"
   J'ai vu dans la crèche
    un petit enfant
   Sur la paille fraîche,
    mis bien tendrement."

3. *"Rien de plus, bergère,*
    rien de plus?
   Rien de plus, bergère,
    rien de plus?"
   "Saint' Marie, sa mère,
    qui lui fait boir' du lait,
   Saint Joseph, son père,
    qui tremble de froid."

4. *"Rien de plus, bergère,*
    rien de plus?
   Rien de plus, bergère,
    rien de plus?"
   "Y-a boeuf et l'âne,
    qui sont par devant
   Avec leur halei
    ne rechauffant l'enfant."

5. *"Rien de plus, bergère,*
    rien de plus?
   Rien de plus, bergère,
    rien de plus?"
   "Y-a trois petits anges
    descendus du ciel,
   Chantant les louanges
    du Père éternel."

'TWAS IN THE MOON OF WINTERTIME

English Translation: J. E. Middleton

Original words in Huron Indian
by Father Jean de Brebeuf, 1593-1649

Andante

1. 'Twas in the moon of win-ter-time when all the birds had fled, That might-y Git-chi Man-i-tou sent an-gel choirs in-stead. Be-fore their light the

stars grew dim, And wan - d'ring hun - ters heard the hymn:——

Refrain

"Je - sus, your King, is born. Je - sus is born. *In ex - cel - sis glo - ri - a!"*

2. Within a lodge of broken bark
    the tender Babe was found,
    A ragged robe of rabbit skin
    enwrapped His beauty round.
    And as the hunter braves
    drew nigh,
    The angel song rang loud
    and high:——
    "Jesus, your king, is born. Jesus is
    born. *In excelsis gloria!"*

3. The earliest moon of wintertime
    is not so round and fair,
    As was the ring of glory on the
    helpless Infant there.
    While Chiefs from far before
    him knelt,
    With gifts of fox and beaver
    pelt.——
    "Jesus, your king, is born. Jesus is
    born. *In excelsis gloria!"*

4. O children of the forest free,
    O sons of Manitou,
    The Holy Child of earth and
    Heav'n is born today for you.
    Come, kneel before the
    radiant Boy
    Who brings you beauty, peace
    and joy.——
    "Jesus, your king, is born. Jesus is
    born. *In excelsis gloria!"*

ACKNOWLEDGMENTS

Cover: © Sylvain Grandadam, Tony Stone Images

6: Malak from Hot Shots
8: Dan Callis, World Trade and Convention Center
9: Fredericton Department of Tourism
10: Sarah Figlio*
11: Greater Montreal Convention and Tourism Bureau
13-14: Malak from Hot Shots
16: *Return from Midnight Mass* (19th century) color lithograph by Edmond J. Massicotte; Musée du Québec (Patrick Altman)
17: *The Traditional Cake of the Three Kings* (19th century) color lithograph by Edmond J. Massicotte; Musée du Québec (Patrick Altman)
18: Metropolitan Toronto Library
19: Colour Library Publishing
20: St.-Anne-de-Beaupre, Québec
21: Colour Library Publishing
23: Musée acadien, Université de Moncton, New Brunswick
24: E. Otto, Comstock
26-27: Metropolitan Toronto and Region Conservation Authority
28: Toronto Historical Board
29: B. Morgan, Prince Edward Island Museum, Charlottetown
30: Joseph P. Meschino, Hot Shots
33: Comstock

34: E. Otto, Comstock
36: Gibson House, City of North York, Canada
37: Ralph Brunke*
38: Malak from Hot Shots
40: Malak from Hot Shots
41: Black Creek Pioneer Village
42: Sarah Figlio*
43: Black Creek Pioneer Village
44: Wayne Sproul, Hot Shots
46: Bob Clarke, Image Finders
48: Culver
50: Granger Collection
51-52: Bob Longworth
53: Nick Newberry
54: Inuit Tapirisat of Canada
56: Ukrainian Cultural Heritage Village
58: Hot Shots
59: Ukrainian Museum of Canada, Saskatoon, Saskatchewan
60: Andrew Sikorsky
61: Andrew Sikorsky*
62: Ukrainian Cultural and Educational Centre
63-64: Ukrainian Cultural Heritage Village
65-69: Yoshi Miyake*

Advent calendar: Yoshi Miyake*
Recipe cards: WORLD BOOK photos by Dale DeBolt*
Music: Jonathan Norton*

All entries marked with an asterisk (*) denote illustrations created exclusively for World Book, Inc.